T0033305

Women&Work

Hannah Anderson · Missie Branch
Portia Collins · Elyse Fitzpatrick · Joanna Meyer
Jen Oshman · Courtney Powell · Courtney Reissig
Faith Whatley · Amy Whitfield

Women&Work

BEARING
GOD'S IMAGE
AND JOINING IN
HIS MISSION
THROUGH
OUR WORK

COURTNEY MOORE
Editor

B&H
PUBLISHING
BRENTWOOD, TENNESSEE

Copyright © 2023 by Women & Work
All rights reserved.
Printed in the United States of America

978-1-0877-8745-9

Published by B&H Publishing Group
Brentwood, Tennessee

Dewey Decimal Classification: 158.7
Subject Heading: WORK \ WOMEN \ WORK ETHIC

Unless otherwise noted, all Scripture references are taken
from the Christian Standard Bible. Copyright © 2017 by
Holman Bible Publishers. Used by permission. Christian
Standard Bible®, and CSB® are federally registered trademarks
of Holman Bible Publishers, all rights reserved.

Scripture references marked NIV are taken from
the New International Version®, NIV® Copyright © 1973,
1978, 1984, 2011 by Biblica, Inc.® Used by permission.
All rights reserved worldwide.

Scripture references marked ESV are taken from
the English Standard Version. ESV® Text Edition: 2016.
Copyright © 2001 by Crossway Bibles,
a publishing ministry of Good News Publishers.

Cover design by B&H Publishing Group.
Photo by Francesco Nacchia/EyeEm/gettyimages.
Author photo by Madison Wuebben.

1 2 3 4 5 6 • 27 26 25 24 23

For the women of the
Women & Work community,

Women who are known and loved
immensely by the Father,
Who are counted as righteous and
worthy by the Son,
Who are empowered and made resilient
by the Spirit.

You have a calling to fulfill,
A contribution to offer the kingdom,
And a good work to walk in.

He's not done with you yet, sister.
This book is for you.

Acknowledgments

Overseeing this project as general editor was a dream come true and the hardest work I've ever done. This book was a collaboration from start to finish, and I am thankful for so many people who helped bring this to reality.

To each contributing author: Elyse Fitzpatrick, Missie Branch, Courtney Powell, Jen Oshman, Hannah Anderson, Portia Collins, Courtney Reissig, Joanna Meyer, Faith Whatley, and Amy Whitfield. I am so grateful you said yes! It means the world to me that you considered this project worthy of your time and effort and that you entrusted me with your work. Thank you for giving your very best and for so graciously receiving my feedback and edits. You will forever have a special place in my heart.

To the B&H Publishing team and our editor, Mary Wiley, thank you for believing that this message needed to be shared and that the Women & Work team and I were the ones to share it. Thank you for being gracious with your time and wisdom, for answering every question, and for improving the draft in valuable ways. I am so proud to know you, to collaborate with you on this project, and to share our FBC Tallassee roots!

To the Women & Work team, both past and present: Penney Smith, Faith Whatley, Amy Whitfield, Sheila West, Courtney Powell, Madi Wuebben, Casey Speck, Courtney Watson, Erika Blaine, Chloe Riley, Carrie Jones, Whitney Pipkin, Missie Branch, Matt Holland, Claudia Glover, Erica Miller, Liz Hauenstein, Callie Burch, Fernie Cosgrove, Brandi Hamm, and Wendy Simmons. Thank you so much for your support and prayers that carried this project through from the very beginning when the thought of publishing was just a desire on our hearts to actually seeing it completed. Your support and encouragement strengthened me to keep going and reminded me of why this book is so important. Thank you for your dedication to the mission.

To Courtney Powell, thank you for your willingness to go the extra mile with me, for not only being my second set of eyes but also for the constant encouragement and love you gave me throughout this project. I could not have finished without your friendship and help. Moses and Aaron, baby!

To my prayer group at LIFEchurch, Ms. Rita, Kim, Erica, Shelbi, Dorinda, Mary, Jennifer, Diana, Araceli, and Shelley, thank you for strengthening me through your prayers and words.

To my many friends, both near and far who are too numerous to name here, thank you for your prayers, coffee gift cards, Scripture and encouraging words you messaged, and for demonstrating that you cared about this project and believed in me. Those kind words and your support meant more than you know.

To my mom, Barbara Cassady, your constant love and support are a rock to me. I stand because of you.

To my brother, Linc Cassady, your friendship, support, and confidence in me kept me moving forward when I wanted to give up.

To my dad, Danny Cassady, thank you for always believing I could do great things.

To Brent, thank you for giving me the courage to start Women & Work back in 2018 when I knew God was calling me to step out but was too fearful to move forward. Thank you for the many hours, trips, conversations, and sacrifices of both time and money you've made to see this organization flourish. Thank you for caring for the kids in those final editing weeks when it seemed there weren't enough hours in the day. Thank you for giving me the space to pursue all God has called me to with this organization. I'm truly grateful for you and love you.

To Jude, Luke, and Shiloh, you are my joy and crown. How I love you. I hope I make you proud.

To my Savior, King Jesus. All of me for all of You. What a privilege and joy to be Your servant.

Contents

Introduction

"IS THIS IT? Is this all there is to life?" I whispered these questions to my friend between sips of pink sherbet punch and bites of petit fours as we delicately balanced our plates on crossed knees and sundresses. The lightheartedness of baby shower games and the sunlight streaming in the windows behind me only intensified the contrasting agony I felt within.

I felt like I was wasting my life.

I was a stay-at-home mom of a toddler and another boy on the way and yet somehow, in the midst of rose-colored balloons and the smiles of cheerful women all around me, I dared to speak out loud the one question that had nagged my soul for months: Was motherhood all there was for me?

Don't get me wrong. I adored my son and wholeheartedly valued my role as mother. I had fully given myself to the task of training and teaching him and any future children the praiseworthy deeds of the Lord (Ps. 78:4–7). I served my family in the home and supported my ministry husband as well as I knew how. It was everything I said I'd

1

ever wanted. Yet something was missing. The baby shower ended that day, but the wrestling I felt within did not.

The questions I grappled with had less to do with the importance of motherhood (that was a given) and more to do with the tension of stewardship in my life. I was called to ministry as a teenager and went on to pursue both undergrad and graduate degrees in ministry-related studies. Yet my call to serve the Lord vocationally became tangled in the messages I heard spoken to young women. If I *really* wanted to honor God with my life, then the best way to accomplish this was as a wife and mom.

Well, I certainly wanted to honor the Lord, so I dove in fully with this "highest calling," never expecting to desire any other type of work. My husband's ministry was the visible one, and I willfully hid my own spiritual gifts in his shadow, supposing his light would shine bright enough for the two of us. But the command of Matthew 5:16 to "let your light shine before others, so that they may see your good works and give glory to your Father in heaven" was not given only to husbands. Wives are not to silently tuck their gifts away as their husbands shine brightly. Matthew

> "Let your light shine before others, so that they may see your good works and give glory to your Father in heaven." (Matt. 5:16)

5:16 is a command to *all* believers in Christ, both men and women, single or married.

Yet, I had not let my light shine. I didn't even know in what ways my light *could* shine, even as a thirty-something-year-old seminary grad. And many of the women I knew felt similarly. Yes, our lights had shone in the area of childcare in the home, but I began to wonder if I could offer more of myself to God than just my service within the four walls of my house. How might I begin to steward the education, intellect, skills, and passions God had entrusted me with, perhaps in ways I'd never imagined? The Holy Spirit was leading me toward something new and fresh, and the book you're holding in your hands is one evidence of the fruit of His work in me.

What about you? How brightly is your light shining? Are you in a season of life where you are maximizing the gifts and resources God has given you, or are you like I was, with talents hidden away, dimming the glow your life could offer the world?

None of us wants to waste our lives. Yet as women, we tend to live with low-level disappointment in ourselves. The gnawing feeling inside that we could be doing more and should be better women in all spheres of our lives plagues many of us. We desperately want to be more productive like other women seem to be on our screens, and of course, we want to do it all for Jesus. In all our striving, we've missed the joy of actually using the gifts given uniquely to us by God. We've chosen to put down our talents for the urgency of tasks that *have* to be done like laundry or dinner, as if stewarding our gifts were optional. But look where that has gotten us. The guilt, frustration, and questions remain. Am I living out my God-given potential for His glory?

Integrating Your Work and Worship

And how is all of this connected to work? Many of us grew up with the idea of work as a necessary evil. Because we need money to live in the world, paid work must occupy some aspect of our lives. We consider work essential, but it's usually segregated from our spiritual lives or the worship of God. In fact, we tend to view most spheres of our lives as segregated from one another. We have separate boxes for family, church, work, friends, health, hobbies, and so forth, which then fit into larger boxes of either sacred or secular. Unless you serve in a church or do some other work that is clearly ministry, work tends to be placed in the secular box. This compartmentalization and division of sacred and secular have not served us well as Christian women. Notice in the verses below how often the word *whatever* is used.

And whatever you do, in word or in deed, do everything in the name of the Lord Jesus. (Col. 3:17a)

Whatever you do, do it from the heart, as something done for the Lord and not for people. (Col. 3:23)

So, whether you eat or drink, or whatever you do, do everything for the glory of God. (1 Cor. 10:31)

Think of all the things you do during any given day. As women, we often multitask and alternate between family duties, work tasks, or texts with friends throughout the day. These verses call us to worship God through *whatever* we're doing, not just the aspects of life that landed in the sacred box, like church attendance and Bible reading. Every box or category of life we mentioned above is to be lived for God and His purposes.

Romans 11:36 tells us: "From him and through him and to him are all things. To him be the glory forever." Did you notice how many things come from God? *All things.* "All things" includes not only the sacred box, but it even encompasses the secular one as well. Now is the time to mentally reach into that secular box, grab your work category with two hands, and move it over into the sacred.

Better yet, dump out the contents of the secular box altogether and find a larger sacred box because *all things* come from God. Look at the next phrase in the verse. All things are to be accomplished *through Him* with the power we receive from His Spirit. This even applies to our work. And all of this is ultimately meant to be offered back *to Him* from our hearts as worship. From Him, through Him, and to Him—all things intended for His glory and purposes.

> All things are to be accomplished *through Him* with the power we receive from His Spirit. This even applies to our work. And all of this is ultimately meant to be offered back *to Him* from our hearts as worship. From Him, through Him, and to Him—all things intended for His glory and purposes.

The apostle Paul gives us a definition of worship in Romans 12:1, the verse that follows 11:36 above: "Therefore, brothers and sisters, in view of the mercies of God, I urge you to present your bodies as a living sacrifice, holy and pleasing to God; this is your true worship."

Through Paul, the Holy Spirit is imploring us not to waste a second of our lives. You as a woman, made in God's image, dwelling in a female body, are wholly meant to live for Him. The things we do with our hands, feet, mind, eyes, and all of the other parts of our bodies can be fully spent for our highest purpose: glorifying our worthy God! It's all a matter of the heart. You can worship God through the use of your hands as you type emails or make your kids' lunches. Your feet can now worship God as you walk the floors of the hospital to assist patients. Your mind can worship God as you prepare lesson plans for your third-grade students. And your eyes can now worship God when you paint a beautiful canvas, imaging your Maker as you create.

> The things we do with our hands, feet, mind, eyes, and all of the other parts of our bodies can be fully spent for our highest purpose: glorifying our worthy God!

Whatever vocation God has called you to is now sacred work, carried out in a body that is meant to be offered to Him every moment of every day. You, as a woman, have been given unique skills, talents, passions, and influence that God requires you to steward well, even through your work. Your contribution to the world matters. How brightly your light shines is of great significance. The way you spend your time and the tasks you carry out are now a part of His grand kingdom purposes as you offer it back to Him. As we yield all things to Him, including our work, our lives will never be wasted. He makes every moment count!

As I look back at the conversation my friend and I had that day at the baby shower, I never could have imagined how the Lord would use those questions I agonized over. The work I was doing in the home with my children was also sacred work, but what I see now is that He was using the restlessness I felt during that season to stir within my heart a vision of how He wanted to use my gifts in even broader ways. Those were the beginning pangs of how Women & Work, the nonprofit organization, was birthed, and ultimately, the beginning of this book.

> Whatever vocation God has called you to is now sacred work, carried out in a body that is meant to be offered to Him every moment of every day.

My Heart for You

Lastly, dear reader, I want you to know there are few things I would elevate above the joy of knowing that this work you hold in your hands actually meets you where you are and propels you forward into all the fullness of God's call on your life. My prayer is that these pages and paragraphs, sentences and words, will be powerfully used by the Spirit of God in your heart to both convince you and compel you to not waste another minute of your life on anything but King Jesus. May you set apart Christ as Lord in your heart, choose to honor and image Him to the world through your work, and leverage your unique potential for His glory.

—Courtney Moore
Founder and President, Women & Work

Chapter 1

The Creation Mandate, Great Commission, and Your Work

Elyse Fitzpatrick

WORK. WHAT'S YOUR UNDERSTANDING of that word? What's your initial response to it? Sometimes when I hear the term, I respond with a groaning sigh, such as when I've begun a writing project, and the words and ideas won't seem to form. Inwardly I complain, *When will this work finally be completed?* At other times, the term conjures up feelings of purpose and excitement, such as when a writing assignment is going so well that my fingers on the keyboard can't keep up with the thoughts coursing through my mind. Some of us face what feels like days of meaningless drudgery. Others look over their frenetic schedule, see no break in sight, and wonder, *When will I get some time to just breathe?*

As I'm writing this, it's the beginning of summer and everyone seems to be posting pictures of exotic beaches and majestic mountains. And I am here looking at my computer screen. I'm just like you. At times, I love my work; other times, it's physically painful. There are times I don't understand why my computer just ate my entire writing project, and other times I send off that final copy via email and am glad I didn't have to go out to print and ship it. Sometimes I am fully convinced the work I'm doing has meaning (like right now), and other times my best plans for making dinner turn out to be a giant waste of time (and food).

Since work is part of our lives and can be such a source of both frustration and joy, it's good that we're taking time to gain an understanding of its place in our lives, particularly as women, and in two key passages from the Bible that define it for us. But first, here's my premise:

- Work is good.
- Work is fallen.
- Work is redeemed.
- Work is eternal.

Let's take a moment to unpack these four principles.

Work Is Good

When done for the right reasons, work is virtuous and praiseworthy. We know that work is good because God is a worker. Not only was He the first laborer, but the New

Testament tells us that Jesus, together with His Father, continued to work, and ultimately Jesus completed all the work His Father had given Him (Gen. 2:2–3; John 5:17; 17:4). Beginning in Genesis, we read that God worked in creating the worlds and the universe. Not only was God working at the beginning, but He also commanded all His creation to work too. He commanded the

> We know that work is good because God is a worker.

vegetation and the animals to grow and produce after their kind. We usually call this work *instinct*, and you can see it everywhere in nature. Plants and animals work continually to multiply "according to their kind" (Gen. 1:21, 24–25). In fact, that's really all they do. Every sort of living creature is commanded by God to "be fruitful, multiply, and fill . . . the earth" (Gen. 1:22). So, of course, they do.

After creating male and female plants and animals and commanding them to work to fill this new world with copies of themselves, God created people. These special beings were to be like their Creator in unique ways. Together they were to represent or image Him and, like Him, rule over "the whole earth" (Gen. 1:26), filling His good creation with replicas of themselves and ultimately of Him.

Then God said, "Let us make man in our image, according to our likeness. . . . So God created man in his own image; he created him in the image of God; he created them male and female" (Gen. 1:26–27). Then He called His female and male representatives to image or mirror Him by working as He did. He blessed them and said, "Be fruitful, multiply, fill the earth, and subdue it. Rule the fish of the sea, the birds of the sky, and every creature that crawls on the earth" (Gen. 1:28).

This command is usually referred to as the Creation Mandate. It is called that because, in it, God set forth His will that these image-bearing creatures would be workers like Him. As equals, the man and woman were to partner together to rule and oversee all He had made, making sure that it flourished and filled every corner of the earth. Then, after the six-day work of creation was complete, God pronounced this wonderful blessing and benediction: "God saw all that he had made, and it was *very good indeed*" (Gen. 1:31, emphasis mine). The plants were very good. The animals were very good. Women and men were very good *indeed*.

Think of that. As a woman, God has said that your creation was very good indeed. Not only that, but He's also given you a purpose, a call, a vocation. You are to be like Him, a source of life and blessing. Perhaps you're wondering how the seemingly insignificant work you do could be a blessing to the earth. Gene Veith Jr. says:

> When I go into a restaurant, the waitress who brings me my meal, the cook in the back who prepared it, the delivery men, the wholesalers, the workers in the food-processing factories, the butchers, the farmers, the ranchers, and everyone else in the economic food chain are all being used by God to "give me this day my daily bread."[1]

We don't usually think of our jobs as the answer to someone's prayer as this quote suggests, but our work is much more significant than we imagine at first. When we consider the broad purposes that God is up to in His world, we begin to see how vital our own contribution is. Our seemingly small work turns out to be a vital piece of the larger puzzle that benefits society. All work has meaning and purpose in God's kingdom. In this way, work is a great good.

> All work has meaning and purpose in God's kingdom. In this way, work is a great good.

We've typically been taught to think that the purpose of work is to make enough money to vacation and then retire well. But this mindset is ill-informed. Part of God's great blessing on the earth is work. The garden of Eden was not an early form of an all-inclusive resort where Adam and

Eve floated down a lazy river with nothing to do all day but sip fizzy drinks. No, it was a place where they were to "work it and watch over" the home God had given them (Gen. 2:15). Like the rest of creation, they were to grow and multiply, but they had one further command: to rule over all they saw and subdue it. That means that every day both Eve and Adam had tasks to do to keep creation on the right track. Sure, the garden where God had planted them was beautiful and perfectly formed, but it needed to be controlled and tamed by their daily labor. They were to work together as loving co-regents in this task. Work was joyous and satisfying and filled with *shalom*, a Hebrew word that speaks of deep peace and flourishing.

Work Is Fallen

Of course, we all know what happened next. Adam and Eve chose to disobey God's command by eating what they were commanded not to eat. They decided to skip over the work they needed to do to become more like their Father, "knowing good *and* evil" (Gen. 3:5, emphasis added). But notice this, when the Lord pronounced judgments after their sin, the place where that judgment fell was primarily in the area of the work they had been given. They lost the painless blessing of work. They lost the easy fruitfulness that had been built into creation. The woman would experience pain in her labor, both in childbirth and also in her relationships with her children and her husband. The man's work would be cursed, and his labor would be painful too. Instead of the earth producing fruit, it would produce "thorns and thistles" (Gen. 3:18). And the fruit it produced would now be born begrudgingly, only after significant sweat and pain (Gen. 3:19). Romans 8:19 tells us that the creation itself is also under the curse and is waiting like us to be set free from its "bondage to decay." In fact, it's even "groaning together with labor pains" (Rom. 8:20–23).

This terrible curse continues even to this day. We see it when our computers crash and when weeds grow in our fields. We see it when we invest in machines meant to lessen our workload such as washing machines or dishwashers, only to have them overflow and flood our homes. We see it when our marriages fall apart or when our children walk away from us. We see it when the business we've labored to build goes up in smoke or is stolen from us by those we trusted. Work is not what it once was. Every part of our labor is tinged with sorrow and frustration. We're groaning while we wait for the resurrection of our bodies, this earth, and our work here.

Our experience with work today is not as it was designed to be. We sigh as we feel the weight of sin's curse. We know that no matter how hard we labor, in many ways our work is futile. It won't last or turn out as we plan, but the good news is that this bleak picture isn't the final one. We can turn our eyes in hope to the One who makes all things new.

Work Is Redeemed

Perhaps work being redeemed is a new concept for you. You've heard that people can be redeemed or freed from slavery to sin through faith, but how could something like work be redeemed? Previously we learned that although God had created work as good, it had been cursed or judged when Adam and Eve sinned. What once had been a source of blessing and joy, would now be difficult and futile. But this, too, has changed in Christ. Paul wrote to the Colossians that even slaves should obey their "human masters in everything." They weren't to "work only while being watched, as people-pleasers," but rather to look at their work as worship of the Lord (Col. 3:22–25). Work now has a reward because God sees how we're laboring in faith and will be sure that we will receive God's blessing for all we do. Work has been set free from the bondage to judgment and futility and now has a purpose: to bring glory to God. Since the fall, the world has been thrown into chaos but through our work, we can bring it back into order. So, when you file that stack of papers or clean out that junk drawer, you're doing holy work.

Even though we still feel many ill effects of the fall, Jesus brought with Him a better perspective on work as well as a new promise. Here's the new perspective and promise:

> Jesus came near and said to them, "All authority has been given to me in heaven and on earth. Go, therefore, and make disciples of all nations, baptizing them in the name of the Father and of the Son and of the Holy Spirit, teaching them to observe everything I have commanded you. And remember, I am with you always, to the end of the age." (Matt. 28:18–20)

This passage is commonly called the Great Commission. While it's normally used in reference to sharing the gospel, it has a much broader scope. What it means is that all our work, no matter what that work looks like today, can be viewed as gospel work. When we teach children to read, we're discipling them to begin to understand this world and their place in it. When we answer phones or draw up schematics for a bridge, we're paving the way for the invasion of the gospel. We're reversing the ill effects of the fall. Martin Luther went so far as to say that the person who repairs shoes faithfully is doing kingdom work. He's loving his neighbor. We are imaging the God who works to bring blessing and shalom to the earth by pushing back against the effects of the fall.

Of course, part of the work that the Lord ordained women to do is "multiply" and "fill the earth" with other image-bearers. Usually, they do this through marriage and their own bodies. This great good can be a source of real joy and satisfaction. For other women, though, marriage or childbirth is not how they will fulfill God's command to make disciples. While the Old Testament was focused on a woman's outward beauty and her ability to birth children, sons in particular, the New Testament's view of womanhood and work is very different. Women in the New Testament are no longer judged by their outward desirability or their fertility. Their worth is not determined by whether they're married or have children. For instance, consider Mary, the virgin; Anna, the widow; Phoebe, Paul's benefactor; or Lydia, a single businesswoman who was Paul's first convert to Christianity in Europe. Today, as before, Christian women receive the sign of the covenant (baptism), just like their brothers. They receive the Holy Spirit and are given gifts to serve in whatever context God calls them to (Acts 1:14; Rom. 12:1, 3–7).

Now, instead of being focused on natural childbirth (although that, as I said, can be a great good), all believing women are to be intent on bringing God's kingdom rule to the earth. They can do that through any avenue of service or work they've been gifted for. Perhaps they'll counsel those who are struggling to believe. Maybe they'll fight human trafficking and rescue women from the sex trade. Perhaps they'll serve good meals at a restaurant, write poetry, or design operating systems. God's good work is as unique as each woman's DNA, and no woman should feel inferior to any other woman because her gifting is different.

The promise that Jesus has given to us in the Great Commission is twofold. First, He claims that He has "all authority." This means there isn't a single snag, hindrance, or problem you'll face today that isn't under His watchful and careful administration for your good (Rom. 8:28) and His glory (1 Pet. 4:11; Rev. 4:11). Even though His love and care ultimately bring comfort, I'll admit that in the moment of disappointments, it can be frustrating that He has allowed this difficulty into our lives. There have been plenty of times I've worked hard to produce something I thought would be helpful to others, only to have it come to nothing. For instance, I once recorded twelve video sessions at a church. This resource was supposed to be used to accompany a book that I had just written. Within six months of the recording, the church was gone, and my work was in a dumpster somewhere. All that work, all those hours, all that prayer . . . for what? Trust me, I'm not speaking from a pain-free position. There are times when we do our best with the right motives, and it all comes to nothing. The only consolation I have at those times is to know that Jesus is sovereignly superintending the outcome. All authority on heaven and earth is His. That means that no matter what shenanigans someone may bring our way, our lives and work are safe in His hands. God sees what you've tried to do in faith and service for Him, and He has promised to reward it.

The second promise Jesus makes in the Great Commission is that He'll be with us forever. As Romans 8:39 assures us, nothing can separate us from His love. Nothing can get in between you, as you labor, and His love. He knows all about work. He knows what it's like to hammer and saw and measure day after day after day. He knows what it's like to teach people who simply don't get it, and who don't even want to get it. He knows what it is to work so hard to build a perfect reputation and then to have that reputation trashed by those who hate you or are jealous. Jesus knows what it's like for you to live the way you're living today. He's done it all. But not only that, He did it perfectly in your place. Find joy in knowing that in all the ways you fail to work diligently, make mistakes, and respond in unbelief, anger, or cynicism, His reputation is your reputation. Before the eyes of His Father, you have the record of the Son, the One who worked perfectly and who demands perfection. He always "lived to please his Father"

(John 8:29). He laid down His life in love for His neighbor. And that's your record today.

Now you don't have to prove your worthiness as a worker or as an employer or employee anymore. If you've put your trust in Christ, all your work failures have been forgiven. That's great news, isn't it? We're forgiven for all the times we fudged on our time sheets, every time we grumbled at an assignment, every time we just went through the motions without really giving it our all. And we're forgiven for apathetically thinking that nothing we do matters or will ever change anything. Jesus paid it all. But we're also justified (Rom. 4:25), which means that his perfect record of diligent work is now ours before his Father. We don't have to strive to earn brownie points by working ourselves to death. We can hold work where it should be, with open palms and gratitude. In Christ, all things have been made new, have been redeemed. Even our work.

> Find joy in knowing that in all the ways you fail to work diligently, make mistakes, and respond in unbelief, anger, or cynicism, His reputation is your reputation.

Work Is Eternal

Of everything I've said so far, you might find this the most surprising. That's because most of us haven't thought about what life will be like in the new heaven and earth. Briefly, the Bible teaches us that when we die, we enter what's called an intermediate state. We're not where we were (in our earthly bodies), and we're not where we're going (the new heavens and earth with resurrected bodies). In this intermediate state, our spirits are with the Lord in the place that most of us call heaven (2 Cor. 5:8). But after Jesus returns, He'll change our bodies to be new ones like His, and this earth and the curse it's groaned under since the fall will be reversed. We'll be back where Adam and Eve were, but so much better. Instead of the garden being one isolated locality, it will be transformed into a city filled with working worshippers that encompass the whole earth (Rev. 21:2). And it will be populated with millions and millions of people who have been redeemed by the work of Jesus.

And what will we do? We'll rule and reign with Christ. Remember how Adam and Eve were to rule over all the earth and subdue it? That's what we'll be doing too. We won't spend our days floating on a cloud or drifting down a lazy river. We'll be busy, but our work won't be doomed to futility. If we set out to learn about a nebula or how to play the music of Mozart, we won't be frustrated. If we desire to paint a sunset or cultivate a particular species of fruit tree, we'll not find it ruined by dried-out brushes or aphids. We will work, but our work will flourish. And in that, we'll learn the true joy of work.

In addition, the work relationships we have with one another won't be marred by selfish ambition, misunderstanding, laziness, or sexism. We'll love one another like sisters and brothers, and we'll be happy at one another's successes, rather than envious or self-hating. Imagine that. The next time you struggle with a coworker, remember it won't always be this way. Then, by faith, seek to love your coworker and serve her, knowing that you've been promised an eternal career filled with flourishing and beautiful relationships. Maybe the way you love that irritating neighbor will be the very thing that will help her believe she can be loved and forgiven too. My sisters, can you see how this is all Great Commission work?

While it's true that work has gotten a bad reputation here on this side of the fall and the new earth, we can rejoice that the things we're called to do today, mundane as they might seem, are actually part of the Lord's grand scheme to glorify Himself and remake this world into a place of flourishing and deep peace. In 1 Corinthians 15:58, Paul wrote: "Therefore, my dear brothers and sisters, be steadfast, immovable, always excelling in the Lord's work, because you know that your labor in the Lord is not in vain."

Here's the wonderful news for every worker everywhere. What we're doing today won't be driven off a cliff to crash and burn at the end of time. No, the work we're doing today will somehow bring God's glorious kingdom to this earth and we'll rejoice in it forever (Rev. 21:24). It's not in vain. No matter if it seems that way right now, know it's not for nothing. That dumpster might be filled with your work, but somehow the Lord is going to use it to bring out and beautify the kingdom to come. So, rejoice. File that folder, make that phone call, design that course, strap into that space capsule, or change that diaper, knowing that the Lord sees what you're doing and will oversee it for the kingdom to come. You're storing up treasure in heaven where God will certainly reward you.

> The work we're doing today will somehow bring God's glorious kingdom to this earth and we'll rejoice in it forever.

Reflection Questions

1. As you reconsider the four aspects of work, which one seems most important to you? Which one is most confusing?

2. How does the thought of your work being important to the world-to-come encourage you?

Chapter 2

Image-Bearing and Your Good Works

Missie Branch

IT'S AMAZING THE LIFE LESSONS that can be gleaned from experiences ten to twenty years ago. One of those memories for me was as an elementary school student in Mrs. Anderson's art class. I loved art class because it gave me the freedom to be as creative as I wanted to be, and on this particular day, the lesson was on symmetry. Drawing was not my gift at all, so even though I loved art, I went into this assignment with low expectations.

Mrs. Anderson instructed us to fold an oversized piece of craft paper in half and paint half of a vase with flowers on it using pastel paints. We were told to only paint on the right side of the fold. Then, when we had finished painting, Mrs. Anderson asked us to press the right half of the paper over onto the left. The sides were meant to mirror each other, and it would create a vase full of flowers. I was skeptical for sure, but to my surprise, it worked. I was elated, and so proud of my art. The shape and details on the vase, the stems of the flowers, the various colors, it was all there. I couldn't believe what I had created.

Just as I designed and crafted my art project with care and beauty, so you and I have also been intentionally and lovingly crafted by our Maker, mirroring Him. You are made in the image of God, and it is from this identity that God brings forth the fruit of good works, not only in your character as He transforms you into the image of Christ, but also in your work.

What Is Image-Bearing?

While my artwork was beautiful to me, it was nowhere near the level of the master creation that occurred in the first chapter of Genesis. The God of the universe, the Creator of heaven and earth, chose to create humankind. He took the time to take a blank humanity and imprint them with Himself so that they would reflect Him to everyone that saw them. Humanity is the crown of His creation made to be like mirrors giving glimpses to others into the heart and mind of God (Ps. 8:4–6). On the sixth day, God looked at the man and woman He had made, and said they were very good (Gen. 1:31). He was pleased with the who, the what, and the why of His creation.

Now take a minute to take this all in. You are His creation. You have been imprinted by Him. That means you have value beyond what you realize and worth instilled in you simply because you exist. As His image-bearer, you were created to image or reflect who God is to the world. We each carry with us certain attributes of His. As humans, we have this distinct privilege unlike anything else He created. We hold within ourselves characteristics of God that only we as humans have been given the opportunity to possess. They are qualities like wisdom, justice, love, and truth. God is all of those things, and now we, as ones who bear His image, can also carry those qualities in us and grow to reflect them more and more to the world around us. We should not take for granted that these were placed in us by the Master Creator. He must have had a plan.

> Humanity is the crown of His creation made to be like mirrors giving glimpses to others into the heart and mind of God.

New Creation: A Life Transformed

Since the beginning of our lives, His image has been on us. Only we as humans have been given the capacity to experience God in this meaningful way. The reality is that glimpses of our identity as image-bearers have always been on display. But once we come to Christ, the image-bearer gets a makeover. Second Corinthians 5:17 describes this change as *becoming new*: "If anyone is in Christ, he is a new creation; the old has passed away, and see, the new has come!" Though we have always been connected to God as His creation and had a special way to reflect Him as image-bearers, once salvation comes, our identity takes on an even deeper, more alive form. We are made new in Christ, renewed women because of this regeneration that has occurred in our hearts by faith. Jesus Himself described salvation as if we are being *born again* (John 3:3). Life as it was will never be the same, even if you can't quite see the changes immediately. In Christ, you are no longer just an image-bearer, but a disciple.

Christians are transformed into a new creation, and the old parts that defiled God's masterpiece are discarded. He removes our old sinful ways, and now we receive the righteousness of Christ. His perfect record now lays the foundation for this new identity we obtain as disciples. The image-bearer gets stamped with Christ's identity, similar to when the two sides of my artwork were folded together. Taking on new characteristics that mirror His, we are forever changed. He has created in us a work of art far superior to what was produced in Mrs. Anderson's elementary school art class.

Along with Christ's righteousness as our new identity, we also receive His Spirit. Ephesians 1:13 says, "In him you also were sealed with the promised Holy Spirit when you heard the word of truth, the gospel of your salvation, and when you believed." Now a permanent fixture inside you, the Holy Spirit acts as your comforter, counselor, challenger, interpreter, guide, and helper. The Spirit is a person, providing the power behind the work being done in our lives and through our lives. I am grateful that the work of being in Christ does not rely entirely on me.

Ephesians 2:10 describes who we are in Christ in even further detail: "We are his workmanship, created in Christ Jesus for good works, which God prepared ahead of time for us to do." When I read these words, they seem to imply that we have value, but what do Paul's words really mean for us? If you were to do a quick search for the meaning of the word *workmanship,* you would find that it is a term that recognizes the high degree of skill used to make a product or to get a job done. The term can also be used to describe the actual pieces created by accomplished artisans expressed through various mediums like songs, sculptures, writings, and even paintings made with pastels. The Greek word used here in Ephesians 2:10 for workmanship is *poiema,* meaning "something made." It's also used in Romans 1:20, where it describes the universe that God made. Our English word *poem* is derived from *poiema.* There is a creative beauty we receive by being God's workmanship. By its definition, workmanship requires an investment of time by a craftsman. You and I are God's uniquely created, carefully crafted art piece—His creation.

New Tools Given for a New Life in Christ

Living as God's actual workmanship who has been created in Christ Jesus will not only impact who we are, but it provides us with a security that will affect *how* we live. Before we became disciples of Jesus and were only image-bearers, our lives still demonstrated worth and value as humans, but we didn't have the ability to truly please God because of our sin (Rom. 8:8). We walked in our flesh, apart from the power of God's Spirit because He had not come to live in us yet. God loves all humanity, but apart from Christ's work of redeeming us back to Himself, humans cannot be accepted before a holy God. We just don't have the capacity apart from His Spirit to make ourselves acceptable. It's like we've been living with broken tools.

> Living as God's actual workmanship who has been created in Christ Jesus will not only impact who we are, but it provides us with a security that will affect *how* we live.

Now that we are in Christ, we can begin to actively believe and rely on the promises of God, which are a kind provision from Him to help us stop navigating through life with the broken tools of working by our own direction, operating in our own strength, conducting our own mission and life agenda. Being His workmanship allows us to no longer be relegated to using that faulty equipment. It's like we're moving from using the damaged tools from the middle school woodshop class to having access to a master craftsman's toolbox. But instead of top-of-the-line drills, saws, and brushes, these new tools are a new identity, a new community within the family of God, a new task to glorify Him through our work, and a new hope and assurance of His coming kingdom. And because the Craftsman is always connected to His masterpiece, we don't just get Jesus's righteousness as our new identity, we get Jesus Himself. His very presence is with us through the person of the Spirit, giving us the grace we need to live and work in a way that now pleases Him (Rom. 8:9–17).

There is a sweetness that comes with inheriting the benefits of the work God is doing. Looking again at this passage in Ephesians 2, we read in verse 10 that God *created* and He *prepared*. God is clearly active. He is at work. The activity going on here is pointing us back again to the work that was done in Genesis when He spent six days creating and also forward to the work He will do at the close of Revelation.

The entire Bible is a display of the powerful work of the true and living God. In it we witness His work of atonement, forgiveness, salvation, rescue, protection, and so much more. God's work is sacrificial and purposeful. It is always motivated by divine love, providing us with a future, a hope, and good works we've been created to walk in. All of this is true of His work in creation in the beginning. When He created man, part of His purpose was for us to be in relationship with Him. With this relationship being primary, everything else in our lives flows from it, everything including our work.

His Work and Our Identity

God's original plan was partnership. From the beginning, He intended to be with us in all of our activities, but then Adam and Eve sinned and separated humankind from Him in Genesis 3. Because of that, He provided us with more of His divine work as Jesus gave His life as the ultimate sacrifice to bridge the divide that our sin has created. He did the work that we could not do to bring us back into relationship with Him. We are only new because of Jesus's work on our behalf that enabled us to become disciples. We have now been gifted with this new identity of being in

Christ and also been given a work to do (Eph. 2:10). God began the work in us and promises to be faithful to see it through to its completion (Phil. 1:6).

Being given this new identity in Christ is no small thing. As a child, I remember seeing a wall chart with a checklist on it entitled, "Who I am in Christ." This list included statements such as: *I am loved, I am forgiven, I am chosen, I am accepted,* and *I am free* with a Scripture reference attached to it. While this may seem a little cheesy on a laminated sign in the Sunday school room, these are truth-filled declarations about the Christian's new identity that is found in Christ. Admittedly, we are as passive in this "new identity" process as Adam was when God fashioned Eve out of his rib. But like Adam, we reap the benefits of the Lord's generous work.

> We have now been gifted with this new identity of being in Christ and also been given a work to do.

Paul also viewed himself as a recipient of his new identity in Christ. In 1 Corinthians 15:10 he wrote: "But by the grace of God I am what I am, and his grace toward me was not in vain. On the contrary, I worked harder than any of them, yet not I, but the grace of God that was with me." Walking in this grace involves drawing on the power of the divine worker within us. This work of grace produces courage where there was only fear, hope where there was only despair, and brings newness and life where there was none before.

Why Am I Here?

Ephesians 2:10 also invites those with this new identity into God's purpose. Let's look at the verse again: "For we are his workmanship, created in Christ Jesus for good works, which God prepared ahead of time for us to do."

With an intentionality and love that only God can possess, He not only saved us and formed us as His workmanship, but we also see in the verse His purpose for us. We have been created *for good works which He prepared ahead of time for us to do.* We have been crafted for work. Good work. His work. Not only has the issue of "Who am I?" been resolved, but now the "Why am I here?" question in our lives has been determined for us as well.

On the day that we painted the vases, Mrs. Anderson made a huge announcement. All of our paintings were going to be entered into a citywide contest. Paintings from across our huge school district would be chosen to be on display in the city's museum of art. The possibility of my painting being on display made this activity feel much more important. It's one thing to create something for myself and my family to enjoy, but quite another for the entire city to observe. Unbelievably, my painting was selected! I was so proud to see my modest painting in a place designed for work so much more impressive, beautiful, and prestigious than mine.

As God's image-bearers, the good work we do every day becomes a beautiful display of God's artistry. He has created us to put Himself on display for others to see, but unlike my painting which was showcased in the art museum, those renewed in Christ have not been created just to be observed. Jesus is the tangible "hands and feet" of the Father. Like Him, we also become for the world the tangible fulfillment of His work. While our lives and actions are being observed by those in our sphere, they should be witnessing an active contribution into God's broader work and purpose that He is accomplishing in the world.

> He has created us to put Himself on display for others to see.

Are Good Works Required?

Does God provide us with a list of activities He expects us to do as part of the *good works* mentioned in Ephesians 2:10? In the nine verses that precede verse 10, we see that nothing we do can earns us salvation. It's all grace through faith, so we know that our good works are not part of the salvation equation. Because we didn't earn it, we can be free from the slavery of seeing our good works as a required to-do list that we must check off. Our good works are not a list of activities like praying and evangelism. Instead, they are all types of things we do that reflect our new lifestyle that has been changed in Christ.

The Bible gives us a broad picture of how we live out these good works. In Romans, we are asked to present our bodies as a living sacrifice. In Galatians, we are given a list of how a Spirit-filled person bears tangible fruit in their lives. Matthew tells us to let our light shine so others can see our good works. Colossians reminds us that whatever we say and do needs to bring God glory. This is a picture of a lifestyle, not a task list. What a relief!

Yes, the life that is committed to doing the good works prepared in advance will be marked by activities like prayer and evangelism, but what is central in this life is the understanding that salvation does not come *from* the work but instead salvation propels us *toward* the work. In other words, we are not saved by our works, but we have been saved to do good works.

> Salvation does not come *from* the work but instead salvation propels us *toward* the work.

A Call to View Work through the Lens of the Kingdom

God has called each of us with a purpose, a work to do. As we have seen from Ephesians 2:10, His plan for each unique individual has been laid out before we were ever made. Your work is unique to you, the way God wired you, and it is a part of this new identity you have been given.

Our good works include all the various ways we work. Most naturally, we see this in the time and effort that we put into serving those in our churches, ministries, and the broader Christian community. But our good works are also seen in our secular work, the work that we do day after day in the marketplace that is motivated by a desire to see God glorified in every sphere. Good works include our domestic work, the work that we do in our homes to be hospitable, generous, and to find rest and to provide respite and retreat. It also includes our personal work as we invest in our own spiritual growth and our physical and mental health. Hebrews 10:24 (ESV) asks the believer to "consider how to stir up one another to love and good works." As Christians spend time with our brothers and sisters in Christ, our work should inspire more good works in each other. As the Christian rubs shoulders with non-Christians, all of our work should demonstrate to them how wonderful our God is.

A lifestyle that produces God's good works has to be lived intentionally because who we are and what we do should be revealing God and His attributes to those around us. Good works reflect His truth. We see His truth expressed by our work being done in integrity, so that we don't compromise for others the reality of who God is and His plan for mankind. Good works reflect God's justice. His justice is displayed in how we relate to each other, the ways we exercise the Lord's judgment, and how we work toward His plan to set things right in a world that is off course. Good works reflect God's wisdom. James tells us that the wisdom of God is not elusive. When our lives include a commitment to prayer, time in His Word, obedience to the Spirit, and the humility to recognize that God's plan is always superior to ours, we reflect good works. With wisdom, our work reflects an understanding of dependence on and trust in Him despite our circumstances or the outcome. Good works reflect God's holiness.

From a commitment to a good works lifestyle comes the purpose that provides meaning for even the most mundane things we do. Now, regular activities like washing dishes, doing laundry, paying bills, writing that paper, cooking those meals, exercising, and serving in church are all infused with

> Good works reflect God's holiness.

value, bringing honor to the Lord. From the simplest work, often seen as unimportant, to things that are public or grand, once it is sifted through the sieve that the kingdom provides, we can see the ways God can use it. Good works will produce in us fruit for others to experience. What an incredible demonstration of the goodness that is present in the plans of God. We are His workmanship created in Christ Jesus, and He gave us good works that He prepared ahead of time for us to spend the rest of our lives doing. It is not lost on me that in His graciousness, He uses us. Good works display God's goodness.

Conclusion

I'll never forget how proud my mom was of my painting being displayed in the museum. The work that I had put into it was now on display for anyone who wanted to come and observe. Like any art aficionado will tell you, all art pieces reflect something about the artist. Being the tangible reflection of the creativity of God should mean that the world through us can come to understand where our true value lies. Who we are is grounded in our identity in Christ, not what we do. Our work is a product of our standing with Him, not the basis of it. Who we are, why we were created, our worship, and the commitment to our work is the result of being God's workmanship, created in Christ Jesus. Good works display God's thoughtfulness.

Years later, there are lessons I have learned from Mrs. Anderson's art class. First, I'm reminded of how completely unskilled I felt as an artist, yet I was faithful to complete the assignment. We must do the work that God has given us. We can't know all of the reasons He has assigned it, but He has chosen to use us. Later in life, many of us will be amazed to see the results. Second, the work I do may seem insignificant, but if it was given to me by God, then it is indeed kingdom work. Fame, power, money, platform, likes, and material assets ultimately disappoint. Investing in the work God has prepared specifically for you to do will always display the heart of the true artist. Your identity is secure because it was given to you by the God of the universe who loves you. Your work is significant for the same reason. You are indeed His workmanship, His beloved

> Our work is a product of our standing with Him, not the basis of it. Who we are, why we were created, our worship, and the commitment to our work is the result of being God's workmanship, created in Christ Jesus. Good works display God's thoughtfulness.

image-bearer and disciple. Walk in what He has prepared for you!

Reflection Questions

1. How does knowing you are God's image-bearer and workmanship change your view of yourself and others around you?

2. In this season of your life, what good works do you sense God has prepared for you? What action step can you take today to begin to walk in those?

Chapter 3

Am I Called?

Courtney Powell

I WAS FIFTEEN YEARS old in my childhood Texas home, lying in bed and weeping on the phone with a friend. "What's wrong?" she asked, fairly concerned. I replied through tears, "I am never going to be able to live in Colorado and teach high school. I feel like God is calling me into ministry, and that means I have to die to all of my dreams!"

I had a picture of what I thought I wanted for my life. I would go to college, get an education degree, move to Colorado because it was my favorite vacation spot as a child, and live happily ever after. In high school, I began to take seriously the study of God's Word and because I loved the Bible and people, I was convinced I should alter my path and go into ministry instead. That culminated in the emotional episode described above when I felt the weight of "the call" into ministry and assumed that call meant I would feel the sacrifice of that decision for the rest of my life.

In retrospect, it's impossible to not look back and laugh at this encounter. First, I actually do now live in Colorado. Sixteen years after this phone call, God led my family to join a thriving church plant outside of Denver. I was also correct that I would not become a teacher, but it turns out that I don't actually enjoy the classroom. During the time I was a teacher's assistant, I quickly realized that teaching was not the profession I wanted to pursue. I suppose I was halfway correct as an emotional sophomore in high school—there would be desires and dreams left unfulfilled. But I didn't understand at the time that those little deaths would occur not because of this call to ministry, but instead because I chose to pursue obedience to Christ, which often led me down unexpected paths.

So what was I experiencing at age fifteen? What does it mean to be "called" into something? The word *calling* typically comes with some confusion because it has not been clearly defined with biblical terms and has often been left up to individuals to determine what they mean when they reference it. In this chapter, we are going to look at some of the myths around how the word *calling* has been used and compare those myths with the truths found around this concept in God's Word.

What Is Calling?

Before we can truly define what calling is, I think it's important to establish what it is *not*. The concept of "calling" I had always heard was centered around stories that often described a mystical experience with God. No one could quite pin down *how* they knew they were called to do something, but they still had a confidence and assurance that *what* they were doing was exactly what God had created for them. But what if you don't have that same confidence? What if you want to make a career change that is completely different from what you thought you would be doing? What if you felt called to be a wife and mother but are single and beyond the age of childbearing? Are you disobeying or defying what you were called into? Did you somehow mess up along the way or mistake God?

This type of confusion exists because unhelpful language surrounding the idea of calling continues to dominate the conversation. In this section, I want to examine a few common phrases I have regularly heard throughout my life and combat those with concrete truths found in God's Word.

1. **Myth:** *"I think you missed your calling here."*

   This language implies that you have done something along the way to miss God's plan for you. Maybe you went to the wrong college or pursued the wrong degree. Perhaps you moved to the wrong city or took the wrong job. This combination of decisions somehow means that what God intended for you has gone awry and you have squandered away your years and efforts.

Truth: God is sovereign, and what He has purposed will come to pass.

In Isaiah 14, God reassured the Israelites that His plan to fulfill His covenant to Abraham would not be thwarted. He promised to make them His people and give them a place. His presence would endure with them, even if their enemies (the Babylonians and Assyrians) seemed stronger and their captivity seemed never-ending.

"The LORD of Armies himself
has planned it;
therefore, who can stand in
its way?

> It is his hand that is
>
> outstretched,
>
> so who can turn it back?"
>
> (Isa. 14:27)

Take comfort in the fact that there is nothing you can do in your life to detract from God's plan for you, which is ultimately to conform you into the image of His Son (Rom. 8:29). Even in the midst of your own brokenness and sinful choices, God still rules over your life in sovereignty and love, and His will for you *will* be accomplished. The decisions you make along the way will certainly have consequences, but they won't come at the expense of God's plans being fulfilled. God can use even our greatest weaknesses to bring about His plan of restoration for the world. If He did it for the people of Israel, rest assured, He will do the same for you.

2. **Myth:** *"The call to _____ is the highest calling for a believer."*

Most of us have encountered this saying at some point with the phrases "motherhood" or "being a wife" or "ministry" inserted into this blank. Can there be multiple "highest callings"? What is the highest calling? Am I missing out if I am not a mom or a wife? If God hasn't called me into vocational ministry, is the work I do less valuable or less worthy?

Truth: The call to be a disciple and disciple-maker is the primary calling for a believer.

Every believer is called to follow Christ and obey Him, and so being His disciple is the primary calling for every person, male or female. There is no hierarchy of value in God's kingdom or with His people.

To be clear, this phrase is typically used as a form of encouragement for men and women in difficult seasons. "The call to motherhood is the highest calling for women" is usually stated with the intent to encourage mothers since many often feel unseen, undesired, or as though the training up of their children is time that could be spent utilizing other gifts. The intention of a statement like this is often to build up, but an unintended consequence is that other women who have not and will not experience motherhood often feel put down. Please hear me when I say this: If you are single or barren, you are not missing out on a *higher* calling. Your obedience to Christ and desire to honor His Word is how you flesh out your primary calling of discipleship, that is, learning from Christ and following Him. You are not experiencing a lesser faith or sanctification in your life because you do not have a husband or a child.

"The call to vocational ministry is the highest calling of a believer" is another form of this that is prevalent in Christian culture. "Vocation" comes from the Latin word *vocare*, meaning "to call." People will often use vocation and calling interchangeably, but for the purpose of this chapter, "vocation" is being used synonymously with

a paid career. Every believer is called
into ministry because every believer
is called to make disciples, but not
every believer will do this vocationally.
Vocational ministry is not more valuable or a *higher* calling. Similar to the
phrase on motherhood, this is often
told to pastors and ministers to place an
emphasis on the work they do in order
to encourage them to persevere when
things get hard. However, the way we
encourage one another should not be
built around the premise of lifting the
value and importance of their work
over another profession, as if doing so is
the only way to spur them on. Instead,
our encouragements for one another
should reflect what we see from Paul to
the churches in his epistles:

> I give thanks to my God for
> every remembrance of you,
> always praying with joy for
> all of you in my every prayer,
> because of your partnership in
> the gospel from the first day

until now. I am sure of this,
that he who started a good
work in you will carry it on
to completion until the day of
Christ Jesus. (Phil. 1:3–6)

Paul's encouragement includes
thankfulness for their work in the
gospel and a reminder that God will
complete the work He started. He is
reorienting their eyes to look forward
to a day when their own sanctification will be complete. The best way to
encourage those around us is not by
unintentionally putting others down,
but by building one another up in love
and reminding one another of their end
goal in Christ.

There is not an indicator in all of
Scripture that a paid ministry position is of higher *value* than a faithful
believer whose work is outside of the
church. Instead, there are admonitions
to all believers to be faithful (1 Cor.
4:2), to work as unto the Lord (Col.
3:17), and to honor Him in all you do

(1 Cor. 15:58). All work done unto the glory of God is kingdom work and is valuable in His sight.

3. **Myth:** *"Once called, always called."*

This phrase may not be as commonly heard as it once was, but the concept surrounding it is still the same: If God has made something clear to you and called you into something, that's it. That is the one and only career path for you, and changing it would mean you are either being disobedient to God or you were incorrect about the calling in the first place.

Truth: Vocations and careers come in seasons, and the only calling that is permanent is the call to follow and obey Christ.

This particular myth is a common refrain for those in ministry to hear; however, the idea that changing careers would be foolish or wrong can be prevalent in culture as well. I hold a music degree from a private liberal arts college, and I am so thankful for it. I had a wonderful experience in college and my musicianship and abilities grew beyond my wildest imagination. But guess what? I have never had a career in music. I learned pretty quickly that even though I was gifted musically and loved studying it, it wasn't a viable profession for so, and instead, I shifted into finance and operations—which was a pretty unexpected turn!

I have been frequently asked the question: "Well, why did you study music? Do you regret it?" And I always answer, no. I don't regret it. All learning is a way in which we image God because He is the author of all knowledge and truth. There is no wasted learning in the economy of God's kingdom, even if it isn't something that provides monetary gain. You can have a passion and gifting that you hone and enjoy without it becoming a sustainable career option. Feel the freedom to grow in your giftedness because God can use your gifts and talents in unique ways to edify the church and the world.

There are plenty of examples from Scripture of people whose gifts were used by God in varying capacities and careers, but perhaps my favorite example is David. In 1 Samuel 16, we see several of the different roles David played:

1. *Shepherd (v. 11 ESV):* Earlier in the chapter, Samuel obeyed God and went to Bethlehem to find Jesse because God told him He had provided a king from Jesse's family. While meeting all of Jesse's sons and trying to discern which would be king, he realized God's choice was not present. David was missing. And the reason? Because he was "tending the sheep."

2. *Anointed King (vv. 12–13):* Once Samuel saw David, it was clear this was who God had chosen to be king. He anointed David in front of his brothers, but then what happened? Samuel left, and David went back to being a shepherd

because Saul was still on the throne at the time.

3. *Musician (vv. 14–19 ESV):* The Spirit of God departed from Saul and he was tormented by an evil spirit. Not knowing what to do, his servants recommended finding someone who was skilled in playing an instrument so that when Saul was tormented again, the musician could play his instrument to soothe him. A servant then recommended David because he was "skillful in playing." Saul sent for David and ended up loving and trusting him. In the last verse of this chapter, David's playing was so excellent that it soothed Saul.

4. *Armor-Bearer (v. 21):* David found such favor in the sight of Saul, he appointed him to be his armor-bearer in addition to his role of playing of the lyre.

In just one chapter of Scripture, we see one person exercising his gifts in four different jobs. This should give us great comfort and rest. God will use the gifts and desires He has given us differently in different seasons. You are not permanently locked into anything other than the call to be obedient to God's Word and His Spirit's leading.

Work and God's Glory

The primary call for every believer is obedience to Christ and growing in His likeness. However, every believer also has a call to work in such a way to promote flourishing in the world. This doesn't mean that everyone will have paid jobs, but all of us have work to do, and this work was intended for us by God from the creation of the world and was part of His plan from the beginning (Gen. 1–3).

Since the day you were born, God has prepared unique and specific good works for you to walk in. The work He leads you to do and the fruit accomplished through it is included in the "good works" of Ephesians 2:10. You have a set of skills, experiences, and expertise that God can use as part of His grand purposes in

> There is no small act of obedience wasted in God's kingdom.

the world. You have the ability to be a light of God's glory throughout the world in whatever season you are in, and His glory is expressed in how we leverage our time and seasons for His glory. There is no small act of obedience wasted in God's kingdom.

How do I know if I am "called" to a career?

We have established that *all* work is good and can be used for God's glory, but that doesn't necessarily help us determine if there is a specific work you should or shouldn't pursue. I am not here to tell you whether or not you are being called into something new or called to stay where you are. Instead, I want to offer some practical categories to pray through that can help you exercise wisdom as you discern your next steps.

A few years ago, my husband and I were trying to determine if we should accept a new ministry position. We loved the church offering the position, and we were in a difficult season in our current church. It felt clear the Lord was calling us *away* from something, but was this new church the place we were being called to *go*? When discussing this with my father-in-law, one of the wisest people we know, he gave us these categories to think and pray through to help us determine next steps. This is my truncated version of what he recommended we pray through, and I have used this formula many times over the years.

1. **Desire:** Do I want to do this? Is the opportunity that has become available something that I actually want to do? Does this position resonate with my own desires and passions? Desire is not the only determining factor. Sometimes God calls us to do things we do *not* want to do (Jonah's call to Nineveh, for instance), but desire can be a helpful tool in discerning what is next.

2. **Gifting:** Do I have the gifts to accomplish this? Am I skilled in the areas necessary to flourish in this role? Desire alone is not enough to discern a career path. It takes skills and determination to accomplish the work required. If your desire to do something far outmatches your skills to accomplish it, you may need to reexamine this opportunity. Not all people are gifted to do all the same things. It's fine to acknowledge this and allow that to be a factor in determining next steps. This doesn't mean you don't work hard to improve or hone in on things that you could grow into, but your own giftings

and limitations should certainly be a consideration.

3. **Affirmation:** Have people around you affirmed that you should move forward with this pursuit? Do you have trusted advisors and counselors that are championing you to move ahead, or are they advising you to proceed with caution? The affirmation of trusted brothers and sisters can be a very helpful tool in processing next steps because God uses people in our lives to help sanctify, sharpen, and grow us.

4. **Opportunity:** Have I been given an opportunity to do this? Desire, gifting, and affirmation are all wonderful tools in discerning a future path, but none of that will really matter if there's no open door for you to actually *do* what it is you'd like to pursue.

A practical way I have used this framework in my own life came when my husband and I were moving from our seminary town into a new state and city for the opportunity for him to become a worship associate. At this point, I had a degree in music and a master's degree in church ministry.

I thought I was called into ministry at a young age, and it seemed like all the pieces were coming together for me to have some sort of career in a ministry job doing music. I had a *desire* to do ministry, that desire was supported by the *giftings* I knew God had given me, and it had also been *affirmed* repeatedly by trusted mentors through my college and seminary years. At that time, I had been given countless opportunities to serve through music, and many of those were paid opportunities. It seemed like the Lord was leading me into a music career that would serve and support my family. But when I married a worship leader, it threw a wrench into all of my plans. Practically speaking, we loved serving together, but it became clear that it was highly unlikely we would ever be able to serve on the same church staff.

I had already begun to grapple with the reality of this before we moved across the country, but it hit me like a hurricane when we actually arrived there. I had a misunderstanding of what it meant to be called. The way I had been taught to understand "calling" was actually not rooted in biblical principles, and I was forced to confront the tension between my primary calling as an obedient follower of Christ and what it meant to be called to do a specific work. The way God made this clear to me was by removing the *opportunities* that had previously been so prevalent.

In this instance, I was able to use the four steps above to discern and determine what was appropriate for my season of life. In submitting to God's plan for that season, my desires began to shift. I was pushed into learning new ways the Lord has gifted me that I was unaware of before, and I developed fresh desires that matched the opportunities I had been given. This formula can be applicable in any season or work as a guide to help discern what the next steps are for you. It may mean stepping into a new career, but it could even mean stepping out of one. Whatever the case, God has given us concrete truths in His Word to guide us and the Holy Spirit to help us exercise wisdom.

When we begin to change our language and understanding around the word *calling* and use the terms in proper, biblical ways, it can radically transform the way we view our own lives and work. We submit humbly to God's plans and His will for us, and we can trust that He is going to transform us in the process and make us more like Christ. He has given you the primary task of being obedient and imitating Him. He has also given you unique giftings and talents that will manifest themselves differently throughout various seasons of your life.

Conclusion

The primary takeaway I hope you leave with as it relates to considering your calling is this: *All work is kingdom work,* and there is no hierarchy of calling in God's kingdom.

Different work choices will have different consequences in your life, but *all* good work is necessary to help build and promote flourishing in the world God made and to help advance God's kingdom to the ends of the earth. God is the one who orders your steps, and He will equip you for your work in every season.

> *All work is kingdom work*, and there is no hierarchy of calling in God's kingdom.

Reflection Questions

1. Have you ever felt that your calling/vocation was less important than someone else's? More important? What are some ways you are going to choose to reorient your thinking around value and "highest calling" in light of God's Word?

2. Are there giftings that could be utilized in deeper or more unique ways? What have you learned about being called and how can it impact how you make future decisions?

Chapter 4

You Are What You Do. Or Are You?

Jen Oshman

"I PROMISE YOU GUYS, I really am funny in English!"

Five pairs of sympathetic eyes looked back at me as my Czech friends nodded their heads reassuringly. I was at my wits' end. Melting down, really.

We had been living in the Czech Republic for about a year. I had been in daily language classes, had a tutor, and was giving all my energy to learning Czech. Despite my every effort, it was coming far more slowly than I was comfortable with.

I didn't know until then how much I relied on my ability to communicate well—how wrapped up my identity was in being a well-spoken woman, a winsome teacher, and just a funny and fun person whenever I wanted to be. For years I had been a Bible study teacher and leader, but of course, in English. I had taken for granted my ability to convey meaning with depth and nuance to my Bible study groups.

Attempting the same thing but in a Slavic language that boasts far more consonants than vowels and employs sounds my American mouth just could not make was a recipe for humiliation. And it wasn't just the mechanics of the language. If you've ever had a friend or coworker who doesn't share your first language, you know how valuable idioms, sarcasm, culture, and traditions are in communication. We discern so much in one another in a simple conversation.

My defeat felt heavy that evening. So much for teaching the Bible in a foreign land. So much for forming sentences above a kindergarten level. So much for being a funny friend!

Like so many in the West, I am prone to equating my worth with what *I can do*. I think we all do this far more than we realize. We subconsciously believe that the value of our lives is measured in the productivity of our days. We want to make a difference, to leave a mark, to point to a list of accomplishments that validates our existence.

Think about it. "What do you do?" is almost always the first thing we ask someone when we first meet them. In our culture, it's what tells us the most about the other person. We get a sense of their interests and skills, their education and income, where they fit within our sphere. And when the question is turned on us, we tend to feel a touch of pride or embarrassment depending on our answer. It's *what we do* that subconsciously identifies us.

Or how many times have you whispered, "How does she do it all?" to yourself as you scroll social media or out loud to a trusted friend in a room full of other women? We see the productivity in another woman's life and we put her on a pedestal. She runs her own business, volunteers in her city, drives her children to every activity under the sun, works out, eats farm-to-table (her farm, of course), and shares her life hacks each morning in her Instagram stories. We marvel at what *she can do*.

Of course, there's nothing inherently wrong with asking, "What do you do?" or wondering, *How does she do it?* And there's clearly nothing wrong with work or productivity or valuing what *we can do*. Indeed, this book rightly celebrates and honors work. But we do well to pause and ponder the intersection of our own identity with our work.

The defeat I experienced in the Czech Republic was the result of me equating my worth with my work. I had made the error of believing that my value is measured by what I can do. I looked to my work instead of my God for my identity.

You and I, as well as our work, were made by God and for God. If that is true, then our work should be done for His glory and not our own gain. And if we work as women made by God and for God, then we can work from a place of rest in Him rather than from a drive to conjure up our own validation through our own human hustle. My hope is that by the end of this chapter we will be convinced that

> You and I, as well as our work, were made by God and for God.

trading in our hustle for the sovereignty and goodness of our God will lead to our own flourishing.

Re-Center Work and Productivity

Work is a good gift, but it is not ultimate. God alone is meant to be the center of our lives, the object of our affections, and the goal of our days. When work takes that place, our souls suffer. In a cultural context that prizes work above God, it's easy for us to do the same. Let's consider the three following truths about us, our work, and our Lord.

First, you and I are not self-made, but made by God and for God. This truth is perhaps the single most important truth we must cling to in all our work. As one of my most cherished Bible verses says, "All things have been created through him and for him" (Col. 1:16). This reality is meant to be our fuel and our comfort. *This* is what's true and lasting and genuinely life-giving.

Second, our work was made by God, and He gives it to us to steward. The apostle Paul says, "We are [God's] workmanship, created in Christ Jesus for good works, which God prepared ahead of time for us to do" (Eph. 2:10). God prepared our work for us before we were even born. And not only that, but He "who started a good work in you will carry it on to completion until the day of Christ Jesus" (Phil. 1:6). You and I can rest in God's sovereignty. He made us, He made our work, and He promises to carry everything to completion.

Third, as creatures made in God's image, the goal of our work is to know God and to make Him known. I love how Jesus shares this simple instruction in his Sermon on the Mount. He says, "You are the light of the world. . . . let your light shine before others, so that they may see your good works and give glory to your Father in heaven" (Matt. 5:14–16). Jesus is the light of the world (John 8:12), and because we are made in His image, we too are lights. We are to work in such a way that people see our Father in heaven in all that we do.

It's Not about You and That's a Good Thing

We live in a self-made age that tells us we are self-made women. Advertisements, movies, and the most-played pop songs tell us we can be whoever we want to be, that we can do whatever we want to do, that we are the culmination of our own efforts. Just hustle hard and make it happen. At first glance, the mottos of our self-driven age seem motivating and cheerful. *You do you! Reach for the stars! You got this! You are enough!*

We cheer one another on in hopes that the energy of our applause will fuel us to the finish line. But here's what we've all experienced at the end of a hard day or in the midst of a tough calling: the slogans, the cheering, and the pump-you-up motivational conferences eventually fall short. The momentary hustle conjured up by our own efforts does not last. Self-made hype runs out. Because you are not God. And neither am I.

When we believe we are self-made and that our work is our own invention and our productivity the result of our own efforts, we function as if we are on the throne of the universe and God is not. We behave as if our work is on us—we must produce, we must get results, we must clamor to make it all happen. But our very nature is to depend on God. When we transfer that dependence to ourselves, we suffer.

In a recent survey of five thousand women who work in ten countries, 53 percent of the respondents said they are more stressed than they were a year prior and nearly half feel burned out. One-third of the women reported taking time off work to tend to their mental health. And more than one-third said their ability to switch off from work was poor or very poor.[2]

The above statistics have myriad causes, no doubt. We know that women balance many pressures from many angles. But in the age of hustle hard, we can safely attribute much of our burnout and despair to a false belief that it's all on us. Soul-deep discouragement naturally flows from our misplaced belief that we are self-made women and we are only as valuable as our work.

Here's some very good news: your life and your work are not actually about you. At first glance, that truth may sting. But sit in it for a minute. Your life, your work, and your results *are not on you*. They are *not on me*. Jesus Himself invites us to breathe a deep sigh of relief and remember that we are finite creatures in the hands of an infinite God. We are not enough. But He is.

> Your life, your work, and your results *are not on you*. They are *not on me*. Jesus Himself invites us to breathe a deep sigh of relief and remember that we are finite creatures in the hands of an infinite God.

I often say, "Burnout is a gift." I prefer to say it to others, but three months ago I had to say it to myself. I had been saying yes to too many projects and sitting at my desk far more than sitting with my family or sitting in sweet and needed rest. Burning out reminded me that I am not enough. Coming to the end of myself taught me (again!) that I don't have to make the world go round. What a relief!

Are you weary? Let us entrust ourselves anew into our Lord's sovereign hands. Hustle is harmful because it insists on being self-sufficient. It's in Christ alone that we find rest and restoration. Your Creator and Savior says even now, "Come to me, all of you who are weary and burdened, and I will give you rest. Take up my yoke and learn from me, because I am lowly and humble in heart, and you will find rest for your souls. For my yoke is easy and my burden is light" (Matt. 11:28–30).

Embrace Your Weakness

Sensing a calling from the Lord that I could not shake, I timidly started a podcast four years ago. It's called *All Things* and the tagline is "looking at events and trends through a Christian lens." In each episode, I unpack a news story and discuss it from a biblical perspective. In our polarized, hot-take, cancel-culture context, I often feel paralyzed by the task and wonder if I really should be doing it. *Did God call the wrong woman? Did I hear Him right?*

During the first season of recording, I was driving with one of my teen daughters in the car. She was curious about the podcast and when I described it to her, she exclaimed, "But Mom, aren't you worried you'll say the wrong thing?"

Without hesitation, I replied, "Yes! In fact, I *know* I will say the wrong thing. And probably many times over."

Her question spoke straight to my deepest fears about my work in public ministry: I was and still am afraid of being wrong, of looking foolish, of accidentally leading my listeners astray. Yes, my child, a thousand times yes. I am afraid of all those things and more. I want my work to be good. And in my flesh, I want it to make me look good.

But the truth is, no matter how educated we are, no matter how well-prepared, no matter how hard we hustle, you and I will always fall short. We are humans who get sick and sin. Moses wrestled with his own shortcomings when God commanded him to confront Pharaoh and lead the Israelites out of Egypt (Exod. 3:10). Moses, burdened with doubt, asked God, *Who am I that I should do this?* (v. 11). He posed all kinds of what-ifs (v. 13) and was convinced he could not be useful to the Lord or His people because he lacked eloquence (4:10). The Lord's firm and comforting reply was, "Who placed a mouth on humans? Who makes a person mute or deaf, seeing or blind? Is it not I, the LORD? Now go! I will help you speak and I will teach you what to say" (4:11–12).

The Lord is our Maker. He knows we are weak. But He does not stand far off or leave us to struggle on our own. What He said to Moses, He also says to you and me, *Go. I will help you. I will teach you.*

The apostle Paul understood this upside-down truth. He was tormented by a "thorn in the flesh" (2 Cor. 12:7) and pleaded with the Lord to take it away. Rather than removing the weakness, though, the Lord told Paul, "My grace is sufficient for you, for my power is perfected in weakness" (v. 9). Counter to our flesh, and counter to our intuition, and counter to our culture, the Lord asks us to embrace our weaknesses, that His strength might be revealed in us and through us. Paul understood that when he felt weak, he was actually strong (v. 10), because of Christ in him, "the hope of glory" (Col. 1:27).

Surrendering our weaknesses requires faith. We must unclench our fists and hand our limited efforts over to the Lord. This pleases Him and brings Him glory, which is precisely what we were created to do. As Moses offered up his weak speech, the Lord met him in it and used miracles to humble Pharaoh and save the Israelites. As Paul offered up his thorn in the flesh, Christ's power was made perfect. What weakness do you need to offer the Lord? He says, *Go. I will help you. I will teach*

> Counter to our flesh, and counter to our intuition, and counter to our culture, the Lord asks us to embrace our weaknesses, that His strength might be revealed in us and through us.

you. And when we do, He will be pleased, and His good gifts will be seen.

Rather than trusting in ourselves, let us trust in the God who made us. Jesus is not looking for perfection. He is looking for women who are prostrate before Him, full of the understanding that we are not our own, that all we have and all we do is from Him and for Him. And here's the crazy truth about God's kingdom: as we surrender our feeble efforts to Him, He uses them for His perfect will, His beautiful glory, and His good and eternal purposes. The fruit of our work multiplies when it's in the Lord's capable and powerful hands. Let us commit ourselves, our work, and our weaknesses "to him who is able to do above and beyond all that we ask or think according to the power that works in us—to him be glory in the church and in Christ Jesus to all generations, forever and ever. Amen" (Eph. 3:20–21).

> Here's the crazy truth about God's kingdom: as we surrender our feeble efforts to Him, He uses them for His perfect will, His beautiful glory, and His good and eternal purposes.

Work from Rest

What if you and I really believed what the Bible says about us? What if you and I grabbed hold of the truth that our worth is not found in what we do, but it's found in who made us, in who died to save us? This would fundamentally change our work. We would no longer hustle for affirmation. We would no longer clamor to make a name for ourselves. Instead, we would shine the spotlight on Jesus. Our work would be a joyful stewardship of what God has already given us. We would rest in our Creator, just as we were made to do.

But how do we *actually do that*? How can you and I practically seek to work for God's glory and not our own gain? I offer five practices that will help you and me work from rest.

1. Start by offering your weakness as worship. Every morning or even before every task, take a minute to pause, remember what's true, and say a brief prayer of confession and worship. Bow your head right there in your workspace and pray:

> *Lord, I am prone to self-glorification and self-reliance. I know I am attracted to the affirmation of others and working in my own strength. But I know that I was made by You and for You. You made this work and*

it's a gift. Thank You for the breath in my lungs, the tools at my fingertips, and even the weaknesses You've given me. Use me, Lord. Help me and teach me and use my work that others may know You and see You in what I do. Lord, You alone are worthy of all honor. Jesus, may Your name be lifted high in this work. Amen.

Of course, tweak that prayer according to your own needs and preferences. The point is to get in the habit of offering your work and your weaknesses to the Lord as an act of worship.

2. Keep God's Word in front of you. Search the Bible and find at least one or maybe a handful of verses that remind you of the truth about you, your work, and your Creator. Maybe the truths about being created by Jesus and for Jesus resonate with you (Col. 1:16). Or maybe verses about God creating your work for you before you were born make your heart sing (Eph. 2:10). Or perhaps verses that magnify the infinite goodness of our God keep your eyes off yourself and on Him (Ps. 115:1). Search the Scriptures, print the verses, and post them on your computer screen, phone screen, office wall, or wherever you will see them to continually reset your frame of mind.

3. Identify your triggers and make a boundary. What circumstances make you feel like your life is only as worthwhile as your work? When do you feel tempted to seek compliments from others? When do you sense the crushing burden of *this is all on me?* It may be when you're sharing your work on social media, or when you're checking your company's bottom line, or when you're in conversations with other women who work in your field. Place a boundary around that context. You may need to limit posting or scrolling. Or you may need to find a friend to review your bottom line or product reviews or follower count. For example, I don't read my own book reviews. I ask my husband to do that and if there's something I need to address, he can let me know. Or maybe when work conversations begin, you can set out to compliment the others in the group to get your mind off yourself and onto what God is doing through them.

4. Engage your community. As followers of Jesus, we need one another. Share your work regularly with your local faith family. Share your needs and your victories. They are your siblings in Christ and they are meant to be a safe place for you to rejoice or mourn. Tell a couple of sisters where you struggle to work from weakness and ask them to stand with you in prayer. Invite your community to help you make much of Jesus in your work.

5. Look expectantly for God to provide. It's true that our God is able to do above and beyond all that we ask or think, so that He might be glorified, seen, and known by others. As you commit your work to Him, look for the many ways He proves strong in your weakness. Be expectant of His provision of energy, teammates, ideas, vision, self-control, or whatever else you ask of Him in need. Be ready to worship Him and thank Him when you see Him come through for you in faithfulness.

An Identity That Never Wavers

The Bible says that we who have surrendered to Jesus are hidden in Him (Col. 3:3). This means that when the Father looks at you and me, dear Christian, He sees His perfect Son. This is the great exchange that allows us to work from our weakness and to rest in Christ alone; Jesus bore our sin, that we might bear His righteousness (2 Cor. 5:21).

There is so much rest and joy and peace here. When our work flows from our weakness, rather than human hustle, we put our perfect, merciful, never-failing God on display. It's not all about us. It's not on us. We are hidden in Him. We have the freedom, then, to work from rest, to work from joy, to give back all that has been given to us in praise of our Father in heaven.

Your identity and mine will never waver because we are securely in the hands of our Savior. Our worth is not dependent on what we do. Our value is not measured by our productivity. We are hidden in Jesus. You and I have value simply because we belong to Him who is infinitely valuable.

It is God who works in you and me, that we might shine like stars in a dark world, pointing others to Him (Phil. 2:13–16). This is our kingdom work: to be hidden in Jesus. To rest rather than hustle. To enjoy the security of being His child. You and I cannot earn that. It's a gift. And it will never, ever be taken away.

> This is our kingdom work: to be hidden in Jesus. To rest rather than hustle. To enjoy the security of being His child.

Back in the Czech Republic, I wanted to be seen as an effective communicator. I wanted my friends to think I was funny and winsome and could teach the Bible beyond a kindergarten level. I had placed my worth in what I could do. And here in the United States that remains a struggle. Each and every day I must remember: I am not what I do, I am the Lord's. I am hidden in Jesus.

Yes, let us labor and strive (work is so often a toil), but let us labor with Jesus's strength and not our own (Col. 1:29). Let us work in such a way that we bring Him glory, not ourselves. Let us walk in weakness, that our God may prove powerful.

When you work, it's not on you. When I work, it's not on me. And that's very good news. Let us rest in this reality and shine our light on the Light of the world. May He be glorified.

Reflection Questions

1. Have you ever experienced burnout from hustling hard and not achieving the results and satisfaction you were hoping for?

2. How might you orient your days and weeks to practically work from God's strength and for His glory rather than your own?

Chapter 5

Bodies of Work

Hannah Anderson

SIX WEEKS AFTER GIVING birth to my first child, I
went back to work as an ESL instructor. It was only part-
time, but even this felt like more than I could handle. My
daughter and I were still figuring out the rhythms of breastfeeding, and no one in the house was sleeping through the
night. We hadn't yet found reliable childcare, so my husband and I developed an elaborate system to make sure one
of us could be with her.

Most days, I'd leave the house with my daughter asleep
in her car seat and head to class. From across town, my
husband would leave the office and race to meet me there.
He'd pull up and jump out of his car. We'd exchange mil-
lisecond hellos and goodbyes and hand off the car seat like
a baton in a relay race. As he drove away, I'd do my best
to collect myself, put a smile on my face, and focus on the

next few hours of teaching. I wanted to exude confidence and convince myself that I had everything under control.

But I didn't have everything under control. I was scattered, tired, and wanted nothing more than to be back home with my daughter. None of my work clothes fit, and I found myself riding an emotional roller coaster almost every day. Even while I was teaching, my new reality as a mother would not be denied; my breasts leaked milk and my bladder called me to the bathroom at inopportune moments. And I very quickly realized that the biggest hurdle to going back to work after giving birth was that I had a body.

Understanding the Challenges

My experience is shared by many mothers. And honestly, I was luckier than most. I only worked part-time. I had a supportive husband. I had somewhat flexible hours. And eventually, we found a friend who cared for our daughter along with her own. But even still, I felt the weight of it all and blamed myself. I believed that I had somehow failed because I couldn't keep up with the demands of both motherhood and work. But with the benefit of eighteen years' hindsight (and two additional pregnancies after which I did not return to work), I can see that my challenges had less to do with me and more to do with a work culture that didn't know what to do with bodies, especially female ones.

The question of maternity leave may seem like it's a question that only affects women who are mothers, but it actually reveals a deeper problem that affects all of us. Yes, the challenges I faced were unique to my calling as a mother, but they were rooted in the fact that I was a physical being. To be clear, my body wasn't the problem; it was working exactly as expected in this situation. The problem was that the systems and structures around me didn't know how to honor it. They didn't know how to honor people embodied as male and female in God's image.

Another example of this tension is the concept of the "success sequence" which promises to help young adults reach financial stability by following three steps. In order, they are:

1. Get at least a high school education.
2. Work full-time.
3. Marry before having children.

The data itself is incontrovertible: young people who follow these steps not only overcome disadvantaged backgrounds, but they also set themselves up for lifelong middle-class stability by their mid-thirties. Not following these steps, on the other hand, predicts higher rates of poverty—which the data also curiously reveals, tends to affect women more.[3] But all in all, this sequencing is the best possible strategy for success . . . for men. After all, *women's most fertile years occur in the same season they're told to be working full-time and building a career.*

And while God does not call all women to motherhood, full-time work, or both, the shape of the "success sequence" signals something larger about how we view our bodies. It includes questions about those who are disabled and differently-abled; questions of vacation time, sick leave, and retirement age. And at the end of the day, the message is clear: If you want to get ahead in your career, you're going to have to deny the reality of your body.

Embodied Workers

In contrast to the way we fragment our bodies from our work, Scripture connects them. When God makes male and female in His image, He gives them bodies fashioned from the physical world. Genesis 2 says that God "formed the man out of the dust from the ground and breathed the breath of life into his nostrils, and the man became a living being" (v. 7). A few verses later, God formed the woman out of the man to indicate

> In contrast to the way we fragment our bodies from our work, Scripture connects them.

that they share the same humanity—the same physicality—even if it manifests in different bodies.

Even more interestingly, Scripture describes human work in relationship to the earth from which we were taken. Genesis 1 frames our work in terms of being fruitful and multiplying and exercising dominion over the *earth*. And Genesis 2 tells us that God put the man in the garden to "work it and watch over it" (v. 15). As a result, he would enjoy the food that the earth gave back to nourish him. Using his body to tend the earth, the earth would, in return, tend his body. The biblical link between human bodies, work, and the earth doesn't mean that we should all be farmers or that cultivating the land is somehow a more noble profession. But it does suggest that our work is deeply embodied.

> The biblical link between human bodies, work, and the earth doesn't mean that we should all be farmers or that cultivating the land is somehow a more noble profession. But it does suggest that our work is deeply embodied.

Whatever work God calls us to do will happen in and through our bodies.

Given this link between our bodies and our work, it's not surprising that sin affects our work in *physical* ways. In

Genesis 3, God told the woman that the curse of sin will "intensify your *labor* pains; you will bear children with painful *effort*" (v. 16, emphasis mine). And speaking to the man, He said, "The ground is cursed because of you. You will eat from it by means of painful *labor*. . . . You will eat bread by *the sweat of your brow* until you return to the ground since you were taken from it" (3:17, 19, emphasis mine).

While some commentators emphasize the gendered nature of sin's consequences, the man and the woman actually suffer under the curse in the same way. In both cases, the work of bringing life into the world will be difficult and unfruitful. And they will experience this pain and futility as they go about their work *in their bodies*. In light of this, my challenges to return to work after giving birth begin to make a bit more sense. Yes, the culture around me didn't know what to do with my body, but I was also wrestling under the futility and brokenness that we all wrestle under. And the fact that I would experience it *in my body* had been predicted thousands of years earlier.

Despite this, we have significant reason for hope; we have reason to celebrate and affirm the goodness of how God designed both our bodies and our work. And we have that hope, in no small part, because Jesus's own work was directly linked to His body. Philippians 2 tells us that Jesus obeyed the Father's call on His life by taking on a body:

by assuming the form of a servant,
taking on the likeness of humanity.
And when he had come as a man,
He humbled himself by becoming
    obedient
to the point of death—
even death on a cross. (vv. 7–8)

In other words, Jesus willingly and eagerly accepted a human body as a way to fulfill His vocation. It was through this *body* that He served, taught, and ministered. It was through this *body* that He died to secure redemption. It was this *body* that was raised again three days later. And it was that same *body* that ascended in power and glory to reign at the right hand of the Father.

And suddenly, things come full circle. Jesus comes into the world to redeem, not just our souls, but our bodies as well. He comes to set us free from the curse that hangs over both our work and our physical lives. He comes to initiate a new creation—a new way of being in the world that unites us together with Him in His own body.

> Jesus comes into the world to redeem, not just our souls, but our bodies as well.

Living Sacrifices

If Jesus's incarnation, death, and resurrection teach us anything, it's that having a body doesn't hinder us from doing the work that God calls us to. In fact, our bodies often help us discern that work—both by what they allow us to do and what they keep us from doing. So that as we present our bodies as living sacrifices, in the words of Romans 12, these same bodies will help us "discern what is the good, pleasing, and perfect will of God" (vv. 1–2).

Here's an example: I am 5' 3". I have been this height since sometime after puberty when I effectively stopped growing. (If rumors are to be believed, I need to enjoy this height now because as I age and my bones shrink, I'll likely lose an inch or two.) While childhood growth charts and my parents' height predicted how tall I might eventually become, I really didn't know until after I stopped growing. Consequently, there was a season in my life when I could dream of being anything I wanted, including a basketball player. But that dream ended when my growth did. It doesn't matter that I never actually wanted to play basketball. What matters is that my body helped direct me away from basketball as a vocation—and quite frankly, any other professional sport. As I tried to figure out what God had for me, that was one thing I could cross off my list.

In a similar way, being embodied as a female offered at least the *possibility* of a vocation as a mother. Being female didn't demand or assure that I have children, but it did open an opportunity that didn't exist for my brothers. And so as I began to navigate questions of vocation, my body helped guide that process. Again, it didn't determine who I would be or what God called me to, but it helped me begin to figure it out. Then as time passed, my body's age also helped direct my choices. Today at forty-three, I'm not terribly inclined to consider a second career as a concert violinist, in part because I lack both the years needed to become proficient as well as the brain plasticity to do so.

These may seem like simple or simplistic observations, but they speak to a deeply practical reality. Our bodies are part of how God reveals our callings in His kingdom. Just as Jesus was called to a specific body in a specific place in a specific time, we are also called to the unique bodies that God has given us. If your body holds the possibility of motherhood and you believe God is calling you to it and providing for it, you'll have to understand it in light of other things He might be calling you to. If you experience chronic illness or other challenges, these realities will inform your calling as well. And while others might not understand your choices, receiving and embracing the body that God has given you, along with its unique limits, can be a way to express faithful obedience.

Beyond these big-picture questions, our bodies direct our daily work in real, practical ways. At the very least, our bodies require nourishment, proper clothing, and rest. This is especially important to remember when we're engaged in physically demanding work or seasons that require long hours. Whether it's cleaning house, carrying or caring for young children, or standing on our feet all day, we must remember that caring for our bodies is not outside of the scope of our work. It is part of our work.

Our bodies also tire and become ill easily. (And that's nothing to speak of how women's monthly cycles tax and exhaust them on a regular basis!) Because of this, we must anticipate and be willing to use sick days. There is nothing noble or godly about "pushing through" when our bodies are crying out for rest and recovery. Instead, aches and pains are the way God has designed the body to communicate its need for care. No more than we'd turn off the smoke alarm when a fire's raging should we ignore these warning signs.

Our bodies also help us determine the scheduling and pace of our work by the simple fact that they cannot exist in two places at once. The digital age invites us to multitask and overload our schedules—so much more work is possible now with email and Zoom. But our bodies remind us of the limits of multitasking. To be fully present in a place and moment requires grounding our bodies there. Remembering this can help us establish healthier boundaries between our public work and private lives and teach us how to resist the temptation of disembodiment.

Even as I write these things, I know that many of you long for them—you long for rest and care and presence— but you also feel completely unable to make them happen. You feel the weight of others' expectations. Your finances and time are limited, and maybe you don't have the support network that you need. Work demands growth, and it feels impossible to care for your body in the way you know it needs. So let me offer this: It is impossible for us to care for our bodies. There is too much working against us. We are too limited. But there is also One who is not, One who has committed Himself to care for us.

And so let me invite you to take your burdens and worries to Him. Let me invite you to trust the One who knows every bit of your body from the hairs on your head to the soles of your tired feet. Trust the God who calls you to not worry about your life, "what you will eat or what you will drink; or about your body, what you will wear" (Matt. 6:25). And instead:

> "Consider the birds of the sky: They don't sow or reap or gather into barns, yet your heavenly Father feeds them. . . . Observe how the wildflowers of the field grow: They don't labor or spin thread. Yet . . .

not even Solomon in all his splendor was adorned like one of these. . . . [Y]our heavenly Father knows that you need them. But seek first the kingdom of God and his righteousness, and all these things will be provided for you." (Matt. 6:26–33)

Trust Him and rest.

Working in Light of Resurrection

In 1 Corinthians 12, Paul uses the metaphor of a physical body to describe how we serve God's kingdom together: "Now you are the body of Christ," he wrote, "and individual members of it" (v. 27). Not only do our bodies matter to our individual callings, but they also matter to the larger work that God is accomplishing in the world. So that as we give attention to our own bodies, we will be better able to serve Christ's body and those we share it with.

One way this will happen is that we will begin to better understand the suffering that accompanies working in and through our bodies. As we acknowledge our own physical limits, we'll better understand the physical limits and the unique needs of our co-laborers, extending to them the compassion that God has shown us. As we learn to juggle the various dimensions of our own callings, we'll extend grace for others, encouraging them to make decisions in light of God's voice, not ours. And as we understand the value of all work, we'll be able to honor each other in the way God intends.

But even as we grow in awareness of being embodied workers, we must realize that not everyone around us shares this perspective. Learning to honor our bodies as God-given gifts will require countercultural choices. It may mean limits on commuting or scheduling so that you can be fully and bodily present in one place at one time. It may mean deferring professional advancement in a particular season of life because your body is busy caring for or nurturing others. It may mean something as simple as resisting the pressure to work overtime so your body can sabbath.

> As we acknowledge our own physical limits, we'll better understand the physical limits and the unique needs of our co-laborers, extending to them the compassion that God has shown us.

But just as much as these limits call us to sacrifice, they also create opportunity. When our work feels stalled by our physical and cultural limits, we have the chance to rethink what we once accepted as normal and respond with ingenuity and invention. For me, this has meant questioning and radically rethinking what surrounding society calls "success" and how to get there. The pressure points of being called to both motherhood and formal ministry have forced me to reimagine what each could look like, including crafting a life in which God's voice (and not other people's) is the loudest one speaking into my decisions and process.

Because even as we struggle through the challenges of being embodied workers, we are not without hope. By faith, we believe that our bodies are valuable. By faith, we believe that God will provide what they need. And by faith, we believe that our bodies will one day be restored to fullness and life. Describing the current state of things, Paul wrote:

> For I consider that the sufferings of this present time are not worth comparing with the glory that is going to be revealed to us. . . . For we know that the whole creation has been groaning together with labor pains until now. Not only that, but we ourselves who have the Spirit as the firstfruits—we also groan within ourselves, eagerly waiting for adoption, the redemption of our bodies. (Rom. 8:18, 22–23)

Ultimately, we can count on the redemption of our *bodies* because Jesus's own body was redeemed from the grave. We trust that just as His body was raised incorruptible, so our bodies will be as well. And having this hope, we move forward, pushing against the tide, seeking to unite our bodies and our work in this life, even as we hope for the one to come. We do so in faith, believing that one day, in these bodies, we will stand before Him in glory, finally free, finally whole.

> By faith, we believe that our bodies are valuable. By faith, we believe that God will provide what they need. And by faith, we believe that our bodies will one day be restored to fullness and life.

Reflection Questions

1. What is one practical choice that you can make today to care for your body and honor your calling as an embodied worker?

2. What is something that you feel unable to provide for yourself in caring for your body as it works? Ask God to provide this for you.

Chapter 6

Don't Waste Your Gifts

Portia Collins

AS A YOUNG GIRL, I remember hearing Darryl
Strawberry's name on television and radio. Darryl's career
as a Major League Baseball player began with great promise, earning him the coveted National League Rookie of
the Year award. Though he continued with great success in
much of his career, even winning several World Series titles,
many have argued that the fullness of his athletic potential
was diminished. Instead of maximizing his natural, God-
given talent, Darryl's poor choices of substance abuse and
legal troubles landed him in a category of wasted potential
and missed opportunities.

Contrast that to tennis phenom Serena Williams,
whose career began and recently ended with demonstrated
consistent hard work and determination. Serena ranked
number 1 in the world in women's singles for 319 weeks

by the Women's Tennis Association. Additionally, she has won over twenty Grand Slam singles titles and is considered one of the greatest female athletes of all time. Her success can be viewed as a result of managing well the talents and resources that God gave her.

The careers of Strawberry and Williams are juxtaposed to one another, offering examples of good and bad stewardship. Good stewardship is a nonnegotiable in the believer's life. God has given us gifts, abilities, intellect, passions, and potential. He has purposed for us not to waste a single ounce of those gifts, but instead, put them to full use for His kingdom purposes. Have you ever considered how you can bring glory to God as a good steward through your work? God has much to say not only about our gifts, but stewarding them for His glory.

What Does the Bible Say about Stewardship?

God Owns It All

You don't have to turn far into the pages of the Bible to discover what God thinks about stewardship. From the beginning, God makes it clear that stewardship begins with Him since He is the creator and owner of all things.

In the beginning, God created the heavens and the earth (Gen. 1:1).

Let's not overlook this seemingly simple verse. At the outset of what God wants us to know about Himself and the world, He establishes that stewardship is a foundational aspect of His kingdom economy. Everything belongs to Him because He created all things. As Creator, He has the right to do with His creation what He wills. In His goodness, He chooses to entrust humans with the task of managing and caring for all He has made. This is stewardship, and it is foundational to being human.

The mere fact that God made us in His likeness as image-bearers illustrates His intent for us as stewards. God created humans as representations of Himself (Gen. 1:27). Just as He rules and sustains the earth, He purposely made men and women to carry out His rule over every other part of creation. Being stewards of God's creation has always been a part of God's initial design for our work. He created us to bring glory to Himself through our stewardship of the earth.

Not only is it God's expectation that we are excellent managers of everything entrusted to us, but God also expects us to do it in such a way that promotes growth. God's plan for Adam and Eve highlights a literal flourishing. As they tended the garden, their work as stewards would produce more food, more human life, more growth. This concept of flourishing as managers is found throughout the Bible. And as we move into the New Testament, we find that our role as stewards is not far removed from what is initially illustrated in Genesis.

Jesus on Stewardship

In Matthew 25:14–30, Jesus illustrates both good and bad stewards. In the parable of the talents, He presents us with three men individually entrusted with possessions from their master. As the master prepares to go away on a journey, he entrusts his servants with varying amounts of talents to manage while he is away. (A talent was a form of currency measured by weight.) To the first servant, he gives five talents, another servant two talents, and to the last servant, he gives one talent. The master expects each servant to make good use of his investment with the full understanding that upon his return, each servant will give an account to him on how well they managed what had been given to them.

While the master is away, the first two servants invest their talents wisely, producing double what they had received. But the last servant took the one talent he had received and acted foolishly. Instead of managing it well to make a profit, he fearfully dug a hole in the ground and hid his talent, earning no return at all. When the master returned, the wise stewards excitedly reported their profits to the master. The servants who made much of what they were given were commended for their faithfulness and fruitfulness. Sadly, the last servant only received rebuke and contempt. Instead of diligently putting to use what was given to him, he allowed fear and the thought of failure to waste his talent.

Through this parable, we learn how serious the issue of stewardship is to God. He gives each of us diverse skills and abilities (and even financial resources) that He fully expects us to put to use. It is not an option to idly let those sit and collect dust. We are to faithfully steward the gifts we've been individually given. We must not look around and compare our skills and abilities with other women, but rather, trust God with what He gives us. Just as the master entrusted different amounts to the servants and measured them according to what was given, so God will justly measure our faithfulness and fruitfulness in proportion to what He has entrusted to us individually.

Did you notice that the servants did not know how long their master would be gone? They could not procrastinate in putting their talent to use. In the same way, we must remember that life is a vapor (James 4:14). Wisdom calls us to make holy use of our time by throwing off distractions and by walking in obedience to God (Eph. 5:15–16). Only then will our days not be drowned by the slow creep of our sinful world, robbing us of our maximum potential for Christ.

The parable also points out how the unfaithful servant was inhibited by fear. Specifically, he was afraid to try and fail. Of all the things I've mentioned, fear is often one of the biggest hindrances to our stewardship as women. How easy it is to remain stuck in the well-worn ruts of our safe and comfortable habits when the Holy Spirit is nudging us to step into something fresh. We can never allow fear to be an excuse for poor stewardship. In fact, fear is the antithesis of faith. The faithful servants in the parable had no way of knowing that their investments would be doubled. But that uncertainty did not cause them to leave their talents on the table. Likewise, we should not leave our giftings from God on the table. Don't be afraid to move forward in faith and do the things your wise Savior is calling you to do. Remember, He is a rewarder of faith (Heb. 11:6)!

> Wisdom calls us to make holy use of our time by throwing off distractions and by walking in obedience to God.

In 2011, I began my professional career in non-profit organizational management at a small university in Mississippi where stewardship was central to my day-to-day job responsibilities. I was a young and vibrant twenty-four-year-old ready to serve her alma mater as the new Annual Fund Officer. In this role, my primary responsibilities included recruiting, cultivating, and stewarding prospective donors to the university. I was the liaison between potential donors and the university, but it was also my responsibility to showcase the university's stewardship of donor dollars.

Although I moved on from working at the university a few years ago, I've been fortunate to continue my career in nonprofit donor development with various agencies. Today, I am blessed to serve donors who give monthly to the faith-based nonprofit ministry where I am employed. Through the years, I've seen a range of financial stewardship, both excellent and poor.

What I have learned through my experience is good stewardship is an integral pillar for successful nonprofit organizations. However, it is not only necessary for thriving nonprofits, but it is also foundational to the believer's life. The parable of the talents reminds us that we must not waste our lives as the untrustworthy, one-talent servant, but instead, step out in faith to make use of our talents and gifts. In the end, we should aspire to hear the same words that were spoken to the faithful servants in the parable: "Well done, good and faithful servant!" (Matt. 25:21, 23).

First Peter 4:10–11 reminds us that stewardship is not limited to finances. What talents or resources do you most notice God has given you? Perhaps you have a special way of making others feel seen and valued, bringing life to those around you. Maybe at work, you notice the Holy Spirit empowering and giving you success at a particular aspect of your job, bringing more growth to your company or coworkers. Or perhaps in the home, you have a knack for not stressing out when guests come, and God uses your gift of hospitality to lift up and encourage your brothers and sisters in Christ. Whatever your giftings may be, let's be reminded:

> Just as each one has received a gift, use it to serve others, as good stewards of the varied grace of God. If anyone speaks, let it be as one who speaks God's words; if anyone serves, let it be from the strength God provides, so that God may be glorified through Jesus Christ in everything. To Him be the glory and the power forever and ever. Amen. (1 Pet. 4:10–11)

What Does God Require of a Steward?

The apostle Paul, who was mightily used by God in the first century and who wrote much of the New Testament, viewed himself as a steward to the assignment God had given him. After his miraculous conversion to Christ on the road to Damascus, God entrusted him with the task of preaching the gospel not only to Jews, but also to the

Gentiles (Acts 9:15). This was his work. In 1 Corinthians 4:1–2, he gives us a behind-the-scenes look at his motivation for perseverance in his calling. He writes, "A person should think of us in this way: as servants of Christ and managers of the mysteries of God. In this regard, it is required that managers be found faithful."

The Greek word for "manager" in this passage is *oiko-nomos* (οἰκονόμους), which translates as "steward," describing one who oversees another person's household or estate. The key aspect for someone like an estate manager is trust. Can the owner of the household trust the one he has placed in charge of his property? Paul viewed himself similarly as God had entrusted him with the charge of sharing *the mysteries of God*, i.e., the gospel (Eph. 3:1–10). Paul knew that to be found trustworthy as a steward required faithfulness.

In 1 Corinthians 9:16–18, Paul says he felt compelled to do what God had assigned him, but even if he did not "feel" this inward urging, he knew he had to carry it out anyway because "I am still entrusted with a stewardship" (v. 17 ESV). He knew that stewards must be found faithful in the eyes of God.

What work has God called you to? You may not have a full-time job as a missionary like Paul did, but God has entrusted you with a specific vocational assignment to carry out. How determined are you to faithfully complete the work He has placed in front of you with excellence, working as unto Him even when you don't feel like it? This not only applies to utilizing your intellect, skills, or abilities, but as a believer in Christ, we can't miss that in these verses, God also commissions us to share the gospel faithfully as Paul did, even with our coworkers. Every believer in Christ is called to a life of evangelism. Let's ask God to help us be found as faithful stewards both to complete our God-given vocational assignment and also to be a light for the gospel with every opportunity He lays before us.

What Does Stewardship Practically Look Like?

Examining the biblical foundation for good stewardship leads us to ask: "What does stewardship practically look like in my own life?" Here are three evidences of good stewards:

Good Stewards Are Humble

One would probably be impressed by a quick look at my résumé or perhaps the highlight reel of my life. I'm a wife, mama, and caregiver. I work thirty-plus hours per week with a women's ministry that has been around for more than twenty years. I am the founder and president of a nonprofit ministry still in its infancy but rapidly growing. I'm a writer, podcaster, and known to cook a mean dish or two in the kitchen.

Honestly though, on most days I feel wholly inadequate for any of these roles God has assigned to me. I am keenly aware of my limitations and weaknesses. And sometimes, I'm very tempted to complain about the level of responsibility God has given me. But I am swiftly reminded this isn't my show. Just like Paul, I realize I am a servant of Christ and am here in these spaces for His kingdom purposes.

God intimately knows every part of my life. In His perfect and infinite wisdom, as Creator, He made me and everything He has given me to steward. I find it nearly impossible to boast in anything relative to my life because it all begins and ends with God (2 Cor. 3:4–6; Rom. 11:36). And not only that but God's sustaining grace keeps me faithful in stewardship (Phil. 2:3–13). Thus, humility is the only appropriate and suitable response I can offer.

The frustration of our work as stewards jumped into motion the moment Adam and Eve thought they knew better than God. Stewarding with humility is acknowledging that we are lowly under-rowers in the great work of Christ. And ultimately, every role and every opportunity that God has called us to in life, though seemingly small, is an intentional and valued component of

> From the garden to the grave, God has purposed our work over His creation, and humility is a necessary vehicle for the excellent steward.

His kingdom. From the garden to the grave, God has purposed our work over His creation, and humility is a necessary vehicle for the excellent steward.

Good Stewards Bear Good Fruit

We are all building something with our lives. The "produce of our lives" is what the Bible refers to as fruit. In the Sermon on the Mount, Jesus says that a person will be known by the type of fruit his or her life produces: "Every good tree produces good fruit, but a bad tree produces bad fruit. . . . You'll recognize them by their fruit" (Matt 7:17, 20). We must note that fruitfulness is not altogether centered on the quantity of how much we produce; rather, on the quality of fruit our lives yield.

The fruitful steward cares about the quality of what she brings to God and is not willfully negligent in service to God, even viewing her work as a means to bear good fruit for Him. Think of it this way—one good, ripe fruit is worth much more than ten rotten pieces of fruit. Doing our work with excellence from a heart of worship to God is one way we can bear good fruit with our lives. In his letter to the Colossians, Paul writes, "Don't work only while being watched, as people-pleasers, but work wholeheartedly, fearing the Lord. Whatever you do, do it from the heart, as something done for the Lord and not for people, knowing that you will receive the reward of an inheritance from the Lord. You serve the Lord Christ" (Col. 3:22–24).

Finally, we must remember that quality fruitfulness only happens when we abide in Jesus Christ. He says in John 15:4–5 says: "Remain in me, and I in you. Just as a branch is unable to produce fruit by itself unless it remains on the vine, neither can you unless you remain in me. I am the vine; you are the branches. The one who remains in me and I in him produces much fruit, because you can do nothing without me." Notice how many times *remain* is mentioned in those verses.

> If we want our lives to produce quality, lasting fruit that demonstrates we are fully utilizing the gifts God has given us, we must be intentional to stay connected to God.

If we want our lives to produce quality, lasting fruit that demonstrates we are fully utilizing the gifts God has given us, we must be intentional to stay connected to God. Perhaps it's taking time to pray more intentionally throughout your day or counseling your heart with Scripture even while you work. Only when we remain in Him will we see the good fruit that promotes the growth and flourishing of those around us.

Good Stewards Are Faithful

As we said before, when it comes to our work, faithfulness to God is the quintessential building block of good stewardship. The definitive statement from the Holy Spirit via Paul in 1 Corinthians 4:2 was: "It is required that managers be found faithful." This faithfulness stems from a heart completely devoted to the master. Our ultimate allegiance must always rest with God. The opinions of man and even the opinions of ourselves massively pale in comparison to how God sees us. Paul knew this to be a fact; therefore, he was confident not in what he thought of himself or what others thought of him, but in what God thought of him (vv. 4–5). Paul was faithful because of his unwavering allegiance to God and His kingdom.

If we follow the same path of faithfulness in stewardship, then, like Paul, we must also be relentless in our allegiance to God. Paul wanted the Corinthian church to understand that God's judgment is what matters most. If we are measuring our faithfulness by the praises or scolding of men, then we are using a far too limited tool. God is the only One who can appraise genuine faith. We should work unto the Lord in all things and gladly look forward to the day when we stand before Him and hear the words, "Well done, good and faithful servant."

All Work Is Kingdom Work

There was once a time in my life when I'd compartmentalize aspects of my work. As a result, I created unhealthy and damaging systems by which I measured the value of my work. There were seasons when I'd give more weight to my work as a professional than I did my work at home. Sometimes I'd convince myself that paid work (punching the clock for forty hours during the week) was more valuable than unpaid work (teaching an online Bible study with friends). Now, I am blessed to view all work as kingdom work. And not only that, but I can see how God calls me to stewardship in various ways, and it is all good for His glory and His kingdom.

At the end of your life, when you look back, what do you hope to see? A life with wasted potential? Or one that recognized all things as coming from a good Father who had entrusted her with kingdom purpose? He has given you everything you need to run the race in front of you in such a way as to win (2 Pet. 1:3; 1 Cor. 9:24–27). Your name may not be Serena Williams, but by faith, your victories of faithful stewardship can be enduring and God-glorifying!

Reflection Questions

1. Take a moment to write down all the ways God has called you to be a steward. (Examples may include parenting, professionally, ministry, and so forth.) How can you better practice humility, fruitfulness, and faithfulness in these areas?

2. Have you ever found yourself compartmentalizing the various ways you work? How does viewing work through the lens of stewardship help you to see that all work is kingdom work?

3. Have you found yourself afraid to do what God is calling you to do? Take a moment to reflect on the areas where fear has hindered your stewardship. Commit to praying about these fears and ask God to help you overcome them.

Chapter 7

Motherhood and the Mission of God

Courtney Reissig

I HAVE FOUR SONS who are all competitive. In the summer months, each of them participates in a summer league swim team. It's equal parts hot and exciting. For twenty seconds, we all hold our breath, waiting to see who will touch the wall first.

The problem is, sometimes the one competing is also desperate to know who will be the first at that wall. So much so, that he loses time looking at the lane next to him. No matter how far ahead he is, he longs to know: *Is he ahead of me? Am I winning?* Inevitably, looking to the left or right slows him down. If he focuses on the goal in front of him (touching the wall), he gets a better time, and maybe even wins. If he worries about the person next to him, he loses seconds on his time, maybe even loses the race.

My kids are not unique in their temptation to glance at the lane next to them. We do this constantly as wives, moms, and employees, don't we? We make a choice that we feel confident about, only to doubt that choice the second we look over at the woman next to us. The struggle with comparison and contentment is seen most clearly when we talk about motherhood and work.

I have worn many hats in different seasons: stay-at-home mom, part-time work-from-home mom, to most recently, full-time working-outside-of-the-home-in-an-office mom. From coordinating work schedules around nap time to scheduling babysitters for morning meetings, I've lived in the unique challenges of these seasons and I still am. But along the way, God has worked truth into my heart about His purposes in our lives.

What Does the Bible Say?

You might be surprised to know that the Bible says much about work, but not much about our modern struggles with motherhood and work. The foundational principle for us as Christians is that God created us to work just as He is a worker. This work began when He created the world and then tasked Adam and Eve to tend to the garden He made for them (Gen. 1–2). As His image-bearers, they joined God in His work of creating more image-bearers and bringing forth more life in creation. Before sin ever entered the world, we had work. And Adam and Eve were co-laborers together.

Interestingly, we can't glean from the first chapters of the Bible what tasks of ruling and subduing are male or what tasks are female. Most cultures have a tendency to divide work sharply along gender lines, but these verses don't draw such specific distinctions. Instead, God gave Adam and Eve a job to do: rule and reign over His creation. He tasked them with being fruitful and multiplying. In both of these tasks, their work had value in the world and value in the family. There are biological distinctions between men and women that naturally divide these tasks; although it takes a man and a woman, only the woman can bear children. But this distinction did not mean that her work in

> To be human is to work, and work is good.

exercising dominion over creation wasn't equally vital and necessary. Every culture and family must discern what works best in their context, but the central truth we can glean from Genesis 1–2 is that to be human is to work, and work is good.

But our work as women doesn't always feel this way, does it? In a chapter on motherhood and work, I think we can all agree that the tasks we do every day often feel futile.

You spend time doing laundry, yet tomorrow's full hamper tempts you to believe your work is in vain. You spend time caring for patients in a hospital setting, yet being away from the home causes you to feel like you're failing your kids. Why is it so hard? Why do we feel this tension so often in our work as moms?

We experience this not because work is wrong, but because we live in a world that is broken.

Once sin entered the world, its consequences directly affected our work (Gen. 3:16–19). What was once beautiful and worshipful is now filled with pain, difficulty, and sorrow. Anyone who has given birth, tried to scrub grass stains out of jeans, or had technology fail them knows that work is hard. And that's not even talking about the struggle with outdoor work.

We often recognize these direct effects of the fall on our work, but the unsettling tension we feel as mothers who work is also part of sin's consequence. As a working mom, I feel pulled in multiple directions. Depending on the context, some might tell me this tension means I am supposed to stay home. As a stay-at-home mom, I struggled to see how my time there had value. In other contexts, I could have been convinced this restlessness meant I needed to work outside the home. But what if both of those contexts are victims of something outside of their control? We are all products of our culture, but we also are people living in a certain time and place. Home and work were not always in competition—and not because all mothers were stay-at-home moms.

How Did We Get Here? A Historical Reflection

The societal landscape of work changed forever at the launch of the Industrial Revolution in the mid–eighteenth century. Prior to this, men and women worked inside the home. Most families were agrarian, and the entire family participated in the work of the farm. The households that did not own a farm ran their own family business in town, where all of the family participated in the work. All of life revolved around the family unit.

Just think of the show *Little House on the Prairie* for a moment. The entire Ingalls family lived and worked together day in and day out. Pa worked on the farm while Ma served on both the farm and in the home. The children were also there in the home, and eventually as they grew, they went to school for a few hours a day. Everyone had a job, and that work was enough to fill an entire day. The Olson family, the Ingalls' friends, lived in town where they owned the country store. Even this family was together, running the family business. Life and work were integrated within the family unit.

In our daily lives, we talk about work/life balance, but their life and work needed no balance. It all merged together. Men largely worked outside on the farm because the bulk of the work was physical and needed the strength that men provided. Women largely worked in the home because many cared for small children before the days of baby formula and disposable diapers. The work of a mom was as physical as it was nurturing. A mom stayed close to home because her nursing babies needed her close to home. A man worked the farm and fields because men possess a physical strength that women often do not.

This all changed with the Industrial Revolution. Men remained in factories for days on end. Women began working there as well, even bringing their children along with them. During this time, work moved from the home and family unit into the marketplace. What was once produced on a small-scale family farm or business was moved to the large-scale factory setting. Handmade items now were machine-produced, and humans were needed to work those machines. The family unit went from a life lived together in one place to one in different locations and directions. As time and technology progressed, people continued to leave the home for work. They moved into urban settings, downtown offices, and could soon travel nationwide via the railroad. Just consider how much our world has changed in the last two hundred years! All of this has had a significant impact on work itself and how we relate to it.

Post-Industrial Revolution and the Homemaker

Fast-forward to the twentieth century when the homemaker became a status symbol—the wife of a breadwinning husband who could provide for the entire family on his salary alone. Prior to this, World War II necessitated women moving out of homelife because they were vital to keep the country afloat during the war efforts. But once the war ended and husbands returned home, men resumed the work that women had been doing in their absence, and wives and mothers returned to homemaking. This was a symbol of a return to normalcy where peace existed instead of war and where families rested in the comfort of suburban middle-class life.

Even though women worked before and after the Industrial Revolution, the difference between the two was the nature of their work. Many of the modern conveniences we use every day in our homes did not exist a century ago. Thus, the work of the home simply does not take as long as it used to. These technological advancements have brought about a conversation regarding work that did not exist prior. Now, men rarely work jobs that women are physically unable to do, yet women still have physical work that men cannot do such as carrying babies and breastfeeding. This shift in the nature of men and women's work has led to the tension that exists with women and work today. Though advancements in technology have helped women (such as baby formula or breast pumps), the reality is that the labor market still has not caught up to a post-Industrial Revolution world where both men and women can do similar work, but do it as truly different beings.

This historical context is important because it helps explain how the tension between motherhood and work exists due to cultural changes, not necessarily biblical ones. If you had mentioned "mommy wars" a hundred years ago and then explained it was between stay-at-home moms and working moms, people would have been confused because every mother was considered a working mom. The distinction between the two is very recent. Biblically, we understand this because we know from Genesis that all of us are workers, but culturally, it falls flat. The desire to work outside the home does not mean you don't love your children or that you want to neglect your calling as a mother any more than the desire to stay home means you don't care about exploring and stewarding your gifts. Women are disproportionately impacted by life in a post-Industrial Revolution society where work and home are sharply divided.

Should I Stay Home with My Kids?

Have you noticed I haven't said anything yet about what the Bible says about whether a mom should or shouldn't work outside the home? That's because the Bible does not give us a step-by-step road map for these choices. Instead, God's Word leads us on the path of wisdom. Both 1 Corinthians 8 and Romans 14–15 talk about the weaker and stronger brother on matters of conscience. These are areas where the Bible does not give explicit commands as it does with murder or adultery. It does not say a mom should or should not work outside the home, nor does it determine an age of her children that deems it appropriate for a mom to "go back to work." It does not say if a mom should earn more or less money than her husband, or if he should stay home or not. As a result, it is a matter of conscience based on wisdom in determining what is best for our families.

What Does Wisdom Practically Look Like?

I remember when I first went back to work outside the home, and I just wanted someone to look me in the face and say, "You're making the right decision." I couldn't shake the overwhelming sense that I was failing my kids. When I dropped my youngest off at pre-K or signed them up for aftercare at school, I felt like I was selling us all short. *Wouldn't they be better with a mom at home full-time? Wouldn't my husband be better for it? Isn't that what God wants for me?*

Maybe you have had those thoughts too. You've searched all over the Scriptures for the magic bullet that says, "You're making the right decision."

If only it were that easy!

Motherhood and work pull at us in ways unlike any other. It pulls at two joint callings—one to steward the gifts we've been given vocationally and the other to steward the ones we have relationally. Let's look at three wisdom principles we find in Scripture.

Walk in the freedom that is yours in Christ.

The first point of wisdom is to understand that God has called us to walk in freedom. Galatians 5:1 (ESV) says, "For freedom Christ has set us free; stand firm therefore, and do not submit again to a yoke of slavery." The Galatian Christians were tempted to see their works as a sufficient means of obtaining salvation. Paul reminded them that God calls them to freedom because Christ paid it all. In the motherhood and work conversation, we are tempted toward these very means of slavery. We might not verbalize that our motherhood choices save us, but our heart responses betray us. We think if we make the right choice, that choice will lead to our righteousness. But Paul says that we are to walk in freedom because Christ paid for us with His very blood, and His blood is what makes us righteous, nothing else. To see our work and motherhood choices through the lens of guilt or shame puts us right back into that heavy yoke of slavery that Christ died to remove from us. Wisdom says to walk in the freedom Christ provides, knowing that our standing before God is not dependent on what we do but on what Christ has already done.

Hard seasons don't mean you should quit.

Wisdom says to keep a long-term perspective on your work and seasons of life. A particularly hard day of motherhood or the temporary mom guilt you feel after a delayed work meeting doesn't mean you've been unfaithful to what God has called you to in motherhood. It might just be hard because life is hard. Galatians 6:9 says, "Let us not get tired of doing good, for we will reap at the proper time if we don't give up." The difficult season you are currently in won't last forever. Your kids will grow up. Your job will change. You will learn new rhythms. Not giving up even when we're tired means we figure out patterns of faithfulness as we work and mother. Hard days or seasons aren't necessarily an indication that the choice to stay home or go back into the workforce is wrong. It might just mean we are being called to an uphill challenge right now. Someday we will run down that hill and reap a harvest.

Throughout this conversation, we must remember that even having the choice to stay home with our children is owing to privilege. Many women in our country and around the world are so busy trying to put food on the table or make ends meet that they can't ask the question of whether they should or shouldn't work outside the home. Income-producing work is a necessity. If you are primarily working unpaid in the home, even if your family has to sacrifice greatly, it is largely owing to privilege that you can make that choice. It's a wonderful privilege, one I am so thankful I took advantage of, but it is still a privilege. Wisdom says that if our requirements for faithful motherhood can't be true for all women, then they shouldn't be required. It is a gift to work in the home if you can and want to, but it is not the mark of faithful motherhood; obedience to Christ is faithfulness.

> Wisdom says to keep a long-term perspective on your work and seasons of life.

Give grace to mothers whose choices are different from your own.

We need to consider that our desire for motherhood is a good desire, and it is not in competition with our desire to work outside the home. The Bible repeatedly speaks of the importance of training our children (Deut. 6:1–9; Ps. 78:5–7). Particularly in younger years, when children need significant nurture and care, it's not uncommon for a mother to pull back from working outside the home in order to care for her children. Once we've made the decision God has led us to make for our family, there is a temptation to feel like the choice we made is the "right" choice for all women. But wisdom says to honor the choices of others, even if they are different from the ones we made. In Romans 14, when Paul speaks on matters of conscience regarding foods that were acceptable to eat, he addresses this judgment that can take place between Christian brothers and sisters. He says,

> One who eats must not look down on one who does not eat, and one who does not eat must not judge one who does, because God has accepted him. Who are you to judge another's household servant? Before his own Lord he stands or falls. And he will stand, because the Lord is able to make him stand. (vv. 3–4)

We must remember that God is at work in many ways in His people's lives, and He does not prescribe one right way to be a woman or a mother. Wisdom says we honor the choices of those who have chosen differently than us and trust the Spirit at work in their lives and in ours.

Can My Life Be Balanced?

The longer I've worked outside the home, the more I think "work/life balance" is elusive. My husband and I have started asking, "Am I faithful?" instead of, "Can I achieve a good work/life balance?" There are seasons when we work more than we prefer, and our homelife suffers. There are seasons when our homelife requires more, and our work takes a hit. But in the balancing act of working and being parents, we have found that walking in wisdom looks like asking if we are being faithful to the Lord moment by moment, knowing that each day looks different than the day before. Particularly when it comes to motherhood and work, the needs

> In the balancing act of working and being parents, we have found that walking in wisdom looks like asking if we are being faithful to the Lord moment by moment, knowing that each day looks different than the day before.

of our children vary so much each day that we can't compare one day's faithfulness to the previous one. We simply wake up each day asking God for the new mercies He promises to provide and walk in faithfulness and obedience with what is in front of us. Every family is different. Every day is different. Every season with our kids is different. We learn to adapt to it as we keep our trust in Him.

A call to view work through the lens of the kingdom

Colossians 3:23 (NIV) says, "Whatever you do, work at it with all your heart, as working for the Lord, not for human masters." That really captures motherhood and the mission of God, doesn't it? How often do we work for the approval of other women? We compare our lives to the mom at the class party because she has the margin in her life to decorate awesome cakes, and we settle for buying them from the store. We feel the need to justify our work both in the home and outside the home when we have conversations with other people because we want their affirmation that we are doing a good job both as a mom and an employee. But Paul doesn't tell us to seek their approval. We only need the approval of one. "Whatever" is pretty all-encompassing. Whether you're in the home or outside the home, work with everything you've got, like God is sitting right next to you cheering you on. That's the call for moms in their work. He made you in His image to work for His glory. You work for Him alone and for His pleasure.

Reflection Questions

1. In what ways do you feel the tension in your work either in the home or outside the home? What lies are you tempted to believe about yourself and your work?

2. Paul says that it is "for freedom that Christ has set us free" (Gal. 5:1 NIV). How are you tempted to fall back into slavery when it comes to your work and motherhood? How does Christ's finished work set you free?

Chapter 8

The Grief and Grace of an Unexpected Career

Joanna Meyer

"WHERE DO YOU SEE yourself in five years?" It was an innocent enough question, the kind it's common to ask in job interviews or at graduation parties. But for me, it turned a weekend bike ride into an afternoon of existential angst.

I was in my early thirties, in the final stretch of the twelve years I worked in college ministry, and I didn't have an answer to that question. "I don't know . . . grad school?" I stammered. I felt paralyzed by my lack of clarity about the future and embarrassed that my uncertainty had been revealed.

My friend Justin meant well in asking that question. He had recently married my former roommate, and filled with a newlywed's optimism, he wondered what I planned for the next season of life. The problem was that I didn't have a plan and was wrestling with the reality that life had not unfolded the way I expected. I lacked imagination for my place in God's world and the courage to act on it.

In the years between my mid-twenties and my early forties, I maintained a hovering posture toward work, hesitantly making plans at each stage of my growing career but holding those plans loosely in case I met a man who would change the trajectory of my life. Trained as a high school teacher, I anticipated working for a few years after college but assumed marriage and family would answer the lingering questions I had about how I would spend my adult life. How wrong I was!

Now forty-eight, I'm still single. By necessity—and God's grace—work has come to play a more significant role in my life than I ever imagined. I often joke that I'm an unexpected career woman, which while true, minimizes the significant work God has done to shape my vision for work and my passion to equip Christian women for influence in public life. The circumstances of my life, and I suspect those of other women as well, require a richer conversation regarding the role we play in God's world. Not checking the boxes of marriage and motherhood pushed me toward a more holistic understanding of work and calling, one that is vital for Christians in any role or stage of life. Along the way, God guided me through seasons of grief into the grace of an unexpected and growing career.

Navigating Seasons of Grief

By my early forties, I thought I had worked through my feelings about singleness. I was moderately content, dating online, and exploring opportunities that were emerging at work.

Then my doctor handed me the results of my blood work during an annual physical. "I think you've grown so accustomed to having heavy periods, that you don't realize how much blood you're losing," she said. The report showed I was severely anemic, a concerning development that launched a multiyear journey through numerous gynecologists' offices, ultrasounds, invasive procedures, and ultimately, a hysterectomy to remove the fibroids that had taken over my uterus. Throughout those years, I bled and I panicked, as my hopes of becoming a mother faded. I spent the months leading up to the surgery crying through church services and dodging baby dedications as the coming loss sank in.

Knowing I would never become a biological mother, took my faith "down to the studs," as they say in home remodeling. Spiritual platitudes offered no solace as I emerged from surgery grieving that I would never experience this part of a woman's design. Unlike friends who were juggling jobs and young children, I had ample space to pursue my career, but my faith was too battered to embrace it.

One of the challenges of that season was realizing that there is no formula for managing grief. In the years surrounding my surgery, God was silent. And no amount of Bible study, counseling, or spiritual direction filled that void. Friends would ask, "How are you experiencing God in this?" and I had nothing to say. I felt awkward mourning childlessness as a single woman and ashamed that I couldn't move myself out of my grief.

I've often wondered if the bleeding woman described in Mark 5 experienced similar despair. Scripture tells us she suffered greatly over twelve years, spending all her money on doctors as her condition worsened. After years of isolation and impoverishing herself in search of a cure, she turned to Christ. "If I just touch his clothes, I'll be made well," she believed (v. 28).

In a similar way, I surrendered to God's sovereignty, the only authentic expression of faith that I had the strength to make. It comforted me to know that Christ, who is described as "a man of suffering, and familiar with pain" (Isa. 53:3 NIV), understood grief. God did not sweep in with a rush of warm emotion, but as I submitted to God's purposes and time line, He led through that difficult season.

As I've watched hundreds of women navigate the tension between their various roles in life, I've been surprised by the diverse forms of grief that we encounter along the way. You may not face the spiritual crisis I experienced, but disappointment tied to your work or relational roles can gnaw on your soul in equally damaging ways. I've watched friends battle fear when their husbands were no longer able to work and they were obliged to rev up their careers. Their grief hit as if they had jumped into a cold lake, stealing their breath and rendering them immobile until they adjusted to the new water in which they swam. Other times grief expresses itself quietly, expressed by younger women who meet me for coffee to discuss the merits of home purchases, promotions, and educational opportunities. They can't hide the excitement of these opportunities but worry they will outpace the men they might date and never imagined making these decisions alone. Or maybe your grief arrives in corporate packaging, when a missed promotion or layoff left you wondering if your work even mattered. Recognizing these disappointments invites us into a deeper conversation with God as we seek to live as our full, authentic selves.

At some point in each of our lives, we will experience grief in our professional or relational roles. Knowing how to navigate these seasons won't eliminate the pain, but will help you trust God through your suffering:

- **Accept the Lord's process and timing.** Don't rush the process. Allow Him to complete His good work in you in His time, not yours (Phil. 1:6).

Resist the pressure to move through pain at a specific pace.

- **Fight the urge to keep up appearances.** Learn to lament, a passionate expression of grief or sorrow. Read Psalms 6, 10, 38, 42–43, or 130, and notice the range of emotions the psalmists express. Biblical figures knew how to mourn, so we can feel the freedom to express ourselves that way too.

- **Protect your heart.** Be selective about who you confide in. As I grieved, I learned that some friends handled the ambiguity of the season better than others. Just because someone is curious about your struggle doesn't mean they should have access to the tender parts of your life. I have also learned to be proactive in social situations that focus on marriage and family. While I delight in my friends' children, I also turn down requests to work in the church nursery and excuse myself from extended conversations about wedding planning.

Embracing My Unexpected Career

By God's grace, He led me through a season of discovery as I emerged from my grief. I longed for biblical principles to guide my career as I was now reminded again of the central role work would play in my life. I joined author Carolyn Custis James in wondering: "Are God's purposes for women only for those whose lives go from early adulthood to 'I do' to the delivery room? Or are His purposes dynamic enough to leave no girl or woman behind?"[4]

What I gained was a compelling vision for work that is rooted in the gospel and flows through every role and season of women's lives. It sparked my imagination for the diverse ways God works in our world, and it led me to see work as a powerful tool for spiritual growth. Having a fresh vision for work brought the resilience and creativity I needed to move on from that hesitant, hovering stance I'd taken toward work, and instead, start stewarding my life in powerful new ways.

> At some point in each of our lives, we will experience grief in our professional or relational roles. Knowing how to navigate these seasons won't eliminate the pain, but will help you trust God through your suffering.

A Gospel as Big as the World

Recently, I ate dinner with a group of women from church. As we traded bites of Korean food, I asked, "Has the teaching you receive in church, women's ministry, or your personal Bible study ever explored why your daily work matters to God?" I was met with a table of blank stares. The four women, who represent a range of life stages, have significant careers in healthcare, nonprofit leadership, technology, and business, yet their discipleship never addressed these areas of influence.

I have found this lack of teaching about work is common among Christian women. Abundant resources exist to cultivate biblical knowledge, relational health, and spiritual disciplines, but few offer an integrated perspective of our roles, one that encompasses the full scope of our gifts and treats our public lives, not just our private lives, as important to God. Christ cares about the state of our souls, but He also cares about every corner of the vast cosmos He created, a scope reflected in Paul's letter to the Colossians. This includes our work. Take a moment

> Christ cares about the state of our souls, but He also cares about every corner of the vast cosmos He created, a scope reflected in Paul's letter to the Colossians. This includes our work.

to skim the following passage and look for phrases that include the word "all" or "everything."

> The Son is the image of the invisible God, the firstborn over all creation. For in him all things were created: things in heaven and on earth, visible and invisible, whether thrones or powers or rulers or authorities; all things have been created through him and for him. He is before all things, and in him all things hold together. And he is the head of the body, the church; he is the beginning and the firstborn from among the dead, so that in everything He might have the supremacy. For God was pleased to have all his fullness dwell in him, and through him to reconcile to himself all things, whether things on earth or things in heaven, by making peace through his blood, shed on the cross. (Col. 1:15–20 NIV)

Then Paul says that, through Christ, God will "reconcile to himself all things." This means that God is at work in ALL THINGS, in every corner of creation, restoring every single part of this world that has been damaged by sin and bringing His goodness, beauty, and truth to the stuff of daily life. God has given us creative abilities and resources, to reform school systems, design efficient spreadsheets, heal the sick, and write stories that inspire. As Paul argues, the gospel that saves us is deeply personal and as broad as the world.

God invites every woman who follows Him, in any role or stage of life, to be part of this grand renewal project. The challenge lies in understanding how to join the process. A simple place to start is to ask two questions: "What about this [situation, setting, or thing] isn't the way God intends it to be?" Or, "How could God's [kindness, peace, love, justice, etc.] increase here?"

I love watching women's imaginations run as they begin to see their unique areas of influence through God's eyes. For my friend Meghen, it means using her sophisticated understanding of tax credits to finance the construction of affordable housing projects in our city. For Dana, a middle manager, it motivates her to change the way her company conducts performance reviews to reduce stress and improve the feedback employees receive. And for Tana, an architectural designer, it inspires her to create welcoming dining rooms at some of the city's hottest restaurants, to encourage

> God invites every woman who follows Him, in any role or stage of life, to be part of this grand renewal project.

hospitality and conversation between guests. The scope and setting of each woman's influence vary, yet each one's work is shaped by this broad view of the gospel.

The world needs who God made you to be. Not in an inspiring, Instagram-post kind of way, but through the specific, often unglamorous, use of your specific skills and resources. Christ's work flows through your private life *and* through your public life as an employee, citizen, and neighbor. How could you help your corner of creation flourish more today?

> The world needs who God made you to be. Not in an inspiring, Instagram-post kind of way, but through the specific, often unglamorous, use of your specific skills and resources.

Work Will Shape Your Soul

In the midst of celebrating this broad vision of women's calling, I acknowledge how hard work can be. Our work, whether we're potty-training toddlers or brewing coffee at a local coffee shop, reminds us of our own limitations and the brokenness of the world. But if we allow God to disciple us through our work, it can become a powerful tool for spiritual growth.

God in the Daily Grind

I crawled into bed last night utterly exhausted from the day. A beloved coworker recently left the company, which means the rest of the team has been scrambling to cover his projects. Between back-to-back meetings, a heavy workload, and a few minutes spent simmering with low-level rage toward a colleague, I hadn't been a model of godliness at work. I'm ashamed to admit that this wasn't the first time the pressures of work revealed the state of my soul.

Learning to see God in the grit of life turns work into a workshop, a place to learn from God and experience His presence. "Christian holiness is not a free-floating goodness removed from the world, a few feet above the ground," explains Tish Harrison Warren. "It is specific and, in some sense, *tailored to who we particularly are.* We grow in holiness in honing our specific vocation. We can't be holy in the abstract. Instead, we become a holy blacksmith or a holy mother or a holy physician or a holy systems analyst. We seek God in and through our particular vocation and place in life."[5]

> Learning to see God in the grit of life turns work into a workshop, a place to learn from God and experience His presence.

Christ understands the unique challenges in your work-place because He worked too. Before He did extraordinary things through His public ministry, He spent thirty years of His life doing utterly ordinary things through His work as a craftsman. I've often wondered what a sinless man would mutter under His breath after smashing His thumb with a hammer. Christ, the carpenter and Savior, understands the circumstances you face and will use your work to shape you into the woman He wants you to be. Your daily work will present opportunities for growth that you could not experience any other way.

I adopted three perspectives and practices to turn my daily work into a tool for spiritual growth:

Recognize His Presence

In conversations with female leaders, the loneliness they feel in work and faith communities is evident. The tendency to see women one-dimensionally, for our relational roles, rather than for the full scope of our influence, leaves many women feeling unknown and unsupported. Donna Harris, founder of the entrepreneurial incubator Builder and Backers and one of the nation's top venture capitalists, describes this struggle to be known: "I participate in a Saturday morning Bible study; we never talk about things like how to behave when you meet a world leader, but I do that regularly. It's very hard to find a peer group and it often feels like the entrepreneur and the CEO part of me gets minimized to make the Christian woman part of me fit."[6]

You may feel lonely if you are the only Christian, woman, person of color (or all three) in your workplace. Friends have shared how difficult travel can be when their idea of appropriate after-hours behavior differs from their colleagues' idea of a good time, or maybe the time you save for your family conflicts with your boss's expectation to respond to emails at any hour of the day. It's not unusual to feel lonely because of who you are or the way you work.

While I believe there are practical solutions to this problem, from highlighting a broader range of women's roles in church contexts to building a stronger relational network for Christian women, these solutions fail to address loneliness at the heart level. This loneliness of spirit can only be soothed by the companionship God offers, that we can thankfully experience in and through our work.

Have you stopped to recognize the presence of the Trinity with you in your work? Take a moment to visualize yourself moving through your work day. Picture participating in every Zoom call, meeting, or coffee break with Christ beside you. The next time your boss gives you feedback that feels hard to accept, acknowledge the Holy Spirit dwelling within you at that moment. Before your next presentation, stop to recognize the Father's pleasure and love for you.

Pray as You Go

Believers throughout the centuries have combined prayer and work. Our earthly work and spiritual work can coexist in our lives today as well, united in a steady stream of prayer. In my life, I pause briefly twice a day to read Scripture and offer a prayer for my tasks. To begin this practice yourself, it may be helpful to set a reminder on your phone at specific times during your workday to pray. Or perhaps your lunch break can serve as a time to turn your heart back to God midday as you consider how the morning went and ask for help for what the afternoon will bring. You might even try breath prayers throughout the day, in which you say a simple prayer with the motions of your breathing. Try it! *Inhale*—"Nothing can separate me." *Exhale*—"From the love of God." Other variations include, "On earth / As it is in heaven," "You are my refuge / And Strength." Repeat the phrase through five to ten cycles of breathing and observe how it calms your heart. Imagine how these prayerful breathing exercises could ground you during a stressful meeting. I love how the seventeenth-century French monk Brother Lawrence describes this blend of prayer and work in *Practicing the Presence of God*: "The time of business does not with me differ from the time of prayer, and in the noise and clatter of my kitchen . . . I possess God in as great tranquility as if I were upon my knees at the Blessed Sacrament."[7]

Accept Christ's Yoke

You may be familiar with the words of Matthew 11:28–30 (ESV), but I'd like you to look at them through the lens of work:

> "Come to me, all who labor and are heavy laden, and I will give you rest. Take my yoke upon you, and learn from me, for I am gentle and lowly in heart, and you will find rest for your souls. For my yoke is easy, and my burden is light."

For the longest time, I thought these verses promised relief through an escape from work. I'd retreat from my crazy schedule, rediscover God's grace, and charge back to the fray only to repeat a cycle of burnout and grace. I failed to see that God was not inviting me to escape my work, but to learn a new way of working. The thought of placing a yoke on a heavy-laden soul sounds anything but restful, but Christ describes it as a place of gentleness, ease, and humility. It's a place of learning from a wiser, stronger partner. We can rest, knowing that when Christ invites us to pair up with Him, He will carry the load.

As you consider new ways of working with God, may the words of Psalm 90:17 ground your work:

> Let the favor of the Lord our God be on us;
> establish for us the work of our hands—
> establish the work of our hands!

Reflection Questions

1. What factors have shaped your perspective on work, specifically your various roles as a woman? How could adopting a broader view of the gospel inspire you in these roles?

2. How have you seen God disciple you through your work? Revisit the three perspectives/practices described at the end of the chapter and identify ways you could incorporate one of them into your daily work.

Chapter 9

Healthy Relationships between Men and Women in the Workplace

Faith Whatley

IS THERE ANYTHING MORE life-giving than words of affirmation from people who love you? There were several men in my life whom God used to influence me and help me grow into leadership as a woman. My dad was the first person who believed in me. He was a farmer's son who attended college and eventually became president of a multimillion-dollar company. He wanted me to have the same opportunities he experienced, and instilled in me both confidence and a strong work ethic. After I was married in 1987, I realized how important that same type of encouragement would be from my husband. At the beginning of our marriage, I started my career as a sales manager for a hotel. This position enabled me to see different aspects of business that I discovered I really enjoyed. My husband was very encouraging and supportive during this time in our young marriage. Later when I gave birth to our premature son, we both felt it was best for me to resign and spend time focused at home without an outside job. One year later, a baby girl was on the way, and we had our hands full! After three years of being at home, I deeply wanted to get back to work. With two small children, I knew I needed a job with flexibility, and God in His providence led me to what is now Lifeway Christian Resources. I served there in varying capacities for over thirty years.

During those three decades at Lifeway, the Lord opened so many doors for me. To summarize my role, I led the women's ministry team in varying capacities for twenty-five of those years. I was the only female employed in the Adult Events sector when we started working with Beth Moore, and I began coordinating women's events all over the country where she taught the Bible. The Lord truly placed me in a seat that would lead to one of the most exciting ministries Lifeway had ever engaged in. God took a young mom and molded her into a leader who could lead women's events with twenty-thousand-plus in attendance.

My experience working with men was probably unique in many ways. Because of my tenure, I was able to grow *up* and *into* management over the years. The men I worked with were extremely accepting of my leadership and voice. I could give you countless examples of men in leadership who mentored me, helped develop me professionally, and championed my giftings as a woman. Between my dad, my husband, and the men I worked with, I count myself as incredibly blessed. My experience has been overwhelmingly positive as a woman in the workplace, but that does not mean that I did not encounter unique challenges along the way.

I am passionate about helping men and women build healthy working relationships with the opposite gender because I had to learn how to navigate those relationships as a young leader mainly on my own, with only a few resources to pull from. I learned to build relationships with pastors, venue managers, truck drivers, production teams, and many male leaders. Eighty percent of the time, I found myself in meetings surrounded by men, where I was the only female. These experiences have helped shape my views of how men and women can work together in not only healthy ways, but in ways that lead to flourishing.

God's Plan for Co-labored Work

God's good design from the beginning was for men and women to work together to accomplish His purposes on the earth. God created the first man and woman and commissioned them in the Creation Mandate to co-labor together as stewards over what He had made (Gen. 1:28). The task of tending the garden and creating a working society could not be accomplished without Adam and Eve working side by side. In God's plan, men and women were meant to work together to fulfill what He had purposed.

Adam and Eve co-labored together as equals. Genesis 1:27 says, "So God created man in his own image; he created him in the image of God, he created them male and female." Both Adam and Eve shared the special quality of being made in God's image, reflecting God's character in their lives. While each were equally important to God in value, dignity, and worth, they were purposely created differently and with distinct roles that reflect particular truths about God. Men and women are not meant to be in competition with one another over these differences, but rather, they should complement one another. As women, we bring to the table a unique perspective that is to be celebrated and valued.

I reflect on how many times the male leaders at Lifeway understood this truth and looked to female leaders for their opinions on issues. They considered their views when making decisions and appreciated how women brought a unique perspective to the situation. Over the years, I watched as women sometimes came into meetings feeling as though they needed to "act like a man" in their leadership.

They believed they would earn respect this way. For many women, this behavior was developed because of prior unhealthy work environments that reinforced the idea that femininity was a weakness instead of a strength. Yet, the unique, feminine ways God has designed you are an asset and strength to the workplace, not something to hide or be ashamed of. Women working alongside men in healthy and appropriate ways can be a benefit to any organization.

Men and Women in the New Testament

The New Testament also shows us examples of men and women who worked together in healthy ways as partners for the gospel. Both Jesus and the apostle Paul co-labored alongside women for the advancement of the gospel.

Luke 8:1–3 tells the story of two women, Joanna and Susanna, who traveled "from one town and village to another" with Jesus and His twelve disciples. These women not only traveled and ministered with Jesus, but they believed in Him so strongly that they supported Him financially from their own means. Jesus wasn't afraid or hesitant to have women serve with Him in gospel work. He didn't view them with suspicion or as a danger. Instead, He valued them and recognized them as His disciples. Because Jesus chose to accept women and welcome them into His work, the cultural status of women was elevated in His day.

And their financial support to His ministry helped provide for their Savior's needs as He completed His earthly ministry.

Mary Magdalene, the woman from whom Jesus cast out demons, was also a huge part of His ministry mentioned in the four gospels. She was present at the mock trial of Jesus, she heard Pontius Pilate pronounce His death sentence, and she saw Jesus beaten and humiliated by the crowd. Mary Magdalene was one of the few women who stood by Jesus until His death. Her heart was to comfort her Lord and Savior who had so thoroughly comforted and ministered to her. She was the first person to witness the resurrection and was sent by Jesus to tell the other disciples. She ministered with Jesus and to Him. Her presence as one of Jesus's most faithful disciples demonstrated her value to His ministry.

In Paul's closing remarks in his letter to the Romans, he sent his greetings to several important

> Paul was a man highly used by God, who valued his sisters in Christ and co-labored together with them as equals, demonstrating for us today that men and women *can* do their best work together in healthy ways, especially as we view one another as brothers and sisters with complementary perspectives, roles, and abilities.

women whom he said were essential in his ministry. Specifically, he named Phoebe, Aquila, Mary, and Junia. In each of these mentions, Paul intentionally spoke words of esteem for each woman. He "commended" Phoebe to the Roman church, specifically called Aquila "my coworker," and described Mary as one "who has worked very hard for you" (Rom. 16:1–7). Paul was a man highly used by God, who valued his sisters in Christ and co-labored together with them as equals, demonstrating for us today that men and women *can* do their best work together in healthy ways, especially as we view one another as brothers and sisters with complementary perspectives, roles, and abilities.

5 Keys for Healthy Relationships for Men and Women in the Workplace

So how do men and women practically work together professionally and continue to build lasting friendships as they strive for the common goal in the workplace? Here are five ways that I hope you will find beneficial.

1. Pray

It is imperative that we pray for each other as we work together. Make it a daily habit to lift up your coworkers and know them well enough that you know how to pray specifically for them. Relationships between believing men and women should be seen as sacred siblings, brothers and sisters in Christ. But even if your coworker is not a brother, make it a point to pray for him. Pray for their spouses, their roommates, their friends, their family. My husband wisely says it is impossible to dislike, have conflict, or think poorly of someone you sincerely pray for. In all of my years of working, I can confidently say this is true.

> Make it a daily habit to lift up your coworkers and know them well enough that you know how to pray specifically for them.

2. Show Respect

In all male/female relationships, men and women must show mutual respect. There will be times you do not agree on decisions or opinions about how to go about the work, but if respect is the foundation of the relationship, you can navigate these disagreements. First Peter 2:17 reminds us to "honor everyone . . ." Honoring your male coworkers is not simply advice, but more than that, it is obedience to an explicit command in Scripture. Regardless of disagreements, choose to honor one another.

3. Set Boundaries Wisely

Because we live in a fallen world and are all affected by sin, it is wise to set boundaries that will help protect ourselves and one another from sinning. Proverbs 4:23 says to "guard your heart above all else, for it is the source of life." Here are some practical boundaries that can help you have healthy, thriving relationships with the men you work with:

- If your employer has guidelines for men and women, it is wise that you follow them. These rules are likely for your protection. There may be practices in place that you find unnecessary or too restrictive, but it will serve you and your organization to submit to the authority of your employer and follow those requirements.

- One of the most common tools for communication in the workplace is texting, but texting without appropriate boundaries can be dangerous. I've heard more stories than I care to count of inappropriate encounters that began with unfiltered texting. Written words can be construed and misunderstood very easily. I would strongly suggest to always read a text you are about to send as if anyone else could read it at any time, and ask yourself if this would cause someone to question the nature of your relationship.

Here are some examples that are innocent but could cause a misunderstanding. Instead of, "Can you talk?" take another second to explain further. "Can you talk about the meeting yesterday?" Or instead of, "Are you here yet? I need to see you," try something such as, "Are you here yet? I need to see you about the employee we were discussing." I would recommend staying away from crass or sarcastic humor that may be unbecoming or joking too playfully. Texts can have consequences and impacts that can be totally unforeseen, so be wise in the frequency and familiarity with which you text your male coworkers.

- The way you present yourself in a professional setting matters. This is a sensitive topic because women often experience the ramifications of being objectified unfairly and inappropriately. However, at the heart of the matter, how you present yourself physically is often a reflection of an inward reality. God asks His people to pursue humility and appropriateness in the way they dress, speak, and act, so presenting yourself in this way is an opportunity to honor God. Be wise and mindful, trusting the Lord sees your heart to honor Him and others.

» Be aware of the potential development of attraction toward a coworker. Galatians 5:16–17 says, "I say then, walk by the Spirit and you will certainly not carry out the desire of the flesh. For the flesh desires what is against the Spirit, and the Spirit desires what is against the flesh." Recognize the signs early and run the other way. If you find yourself drawn to a coworker, pull back and keep all conversations limited to work. Create boundaries that will enable you to work together successfully but leave no room for an inappropriate relationship to form.

» If you have a male coworker who jokes about his wife or begins to share their marital problems with you, stop these conversations, and be clear that this type of discussion is inappropriate. If you are married and find yourself having feelings for a coworker, or if you are single and notice that you have feelings for a married coworker, immediately tell a trusted counselor or confidant so you can begin praying and discerning if working together is a sustainable option. Take those feelings seriously and put measures in place that match the seriousness of the situation. You may end up needing to resign to avoid potential sin. If that's the case, trust that the Lord will provide for you and honor your desire to obey Him.

• If you are managing men and they are married, be intentional to honor their wives. If there is an opportunity to engage with them, be intentional to do so. It can be difficult to be a spouse who has no relational context with her husband's coworkers. If you are able to help ease that difficulty, do so.

4. Lean in to Difficult Situations

I was fortunate to have another wise female leader in my life who was a few years ahead of me who gave me this advice: lean in to hard situations.

When your first inclination is to pull away from a difficult situation or circumstance that feels too hard to proceed through, you most likely should actually lean in to it. So many times after moving toward a hard situation instead of away, the outcome was often better than I expected and easier than my initial fears. This is especially true with male colleagues or supervisors. If you sense there is an issue, lean in and discuss it. Over the years, I met with so many women who shared challenges they experienced with their male supervisors. The tension was so great that it had crippled the work. In most of those situations, there was a communication breakdown and the issue had festered to make it worse than it was in the beginning. Addressing things early on can sometimes prevent many misunderstandings and further relational difficulties.

In regard to leaning in, there is also leading *up* to your immediate supervisor. Leading up means you have an established relationship with your male leaders, and you see an area they need to improve or a situation they need to handle differently. The practice of leading up can be tricky. The timing must be right, and the conversation needs to be respectful. I once sent a text to a male supervisor that was negative in nature, but I didn't know he was about to walk on the stage at an important meeting to speak. My text wasn't received well. However, we had built a strong enough relationship so that he was able to tell me, "Thanks a lot, Faith . . . I was just about to speak to 2,000 people." A good leader seeks to guide others in a way that will inspire their own leadership. These conversations need to be winsome and honoring.

There may be times these types of conversations will not be received well. In that case, my best advice would be to pray for a resolution that will be edifying for your supervisor. Leading up can be intimidating, and it takes courage. You need mutual respect to accomplish it. Be wise in initiating these conversations and prayerful in discerning next steps.

5. Give the Benefit of the Doubt

Give your male coworkers the benefit of the doubt by setting the foundation of your relationship with them with a posture of believing the best of them. This is a distinctly Christian virtue echoed in 1 Corinthians 13:7, "[Love] believes all things." This instruction from Paul applies to the way we view one another, even in the marketplace. As I have gotten older, I've discovered this is one of the most important aspects to having a healthy relationship with men in the workplace.

Unfortunately, I have too many examples of assuming the worst intentions of a male counterpart only to discover that I had misjudged their motives. In one specific instance early in my leadership, I had a partner choose to go with another publisher. I let this decision hurt my feelings, and I believed his intent was to offend me and hurt the organization. I immediately sent an email to him. I still think about that email to this day. I let my flesh go before the Spirit and decided to retaliate against him. I attempted to make him feel foolish for his decision. In retrospect, I realize I misjudged this partner's intentions and took his decision personally when the intent behind the decision was a business decision, not a personal one.

If you will begin from a posture of assuming the best intentions of your male coworkers instead of the worst, it will help your relationships to develop in a healthy way that can grow into something that flourishes and thrives. Healthy working relationships between men and women are not only possible, but they are a beautiful picture of God's command to subdue the earth, honoring God together.

Now after thirty years, I am in a season of retirement and don't work shoulder to shoulder with my brothers every day as I did. Do I miss working? Not necessarily, but I do miss the deep and sacred relationships I had with my coworkers. They are some of my best friends and will always hold a special place in my heart. Many men were my true brothers in Christ, and when I hear of their good, continued work, I miss them even more. Thank you, Bill, Michael, Trevin, Jon, Mike, Eric, Earl, Jeff, Lance, Bruce, Kevin, and many more for helping me grow into a leader that hopefully you wanted to work with as much as I enjoyed working with you. Thank you for always respecting me as a female leader. It did not go unnoticed.

> Healthy working relationships between men and women are not only possible, but they are a beautiful picture of God's command to subdue the earth, honoring God together.

Reflection Questions

1. Are you in a setting where you are contributing to healthy male/female relationships in the workplace? What are some ways you can ensure boundaries are helping those relationships flourish?

2. Do you regularly pray for those you work with? Write out a prayer for the men and women you see at work and set a time to pray for them regularly.

Chapter 10

Developing and Growing Your Gifts

Amy Whitfield

I LIKE TO CALL myself an accidental leader. When I got my start in the workplace, I didn't set out to lead a team or a department, a project or an initiative. I didn't consider that a possible path, and in my particular environment, I saw no real potential for career advancement.

I had three basic goals. First, my husband and I had bills to pay. Sometimes you look for a job because you need one! Second, I wanted to make a difference as part of something bigger than myself. My third goal was to never stop learning. As an Enneagram 5 through and through, I don't need an endgame for the information I take in. I enjoy reading and researching and studying, even if for no other reason than to understand the world around me. What I didn't anticipate was how much my love of learning would enable me to be used by God in the world.

Over two decades later, I'm serving in a job I never dreamed was possible, following a calling I couldn't have even imagined for myself. The path that began in those early years was filled with twists and turns. Many roads appeared to be dead ends but later emerged as a clear way through. Some years rushed by with change, while others lingered with loneliness. Through these varying seasons of either progress or silence, the one common thread was that the Lord continued to grow me, even when I couldn't see it.

Growth as a Christian

Personal development is a hot topic in the workplace these days, with many organizations investing in their employees with training sessions, continuing education, money for books and conferences, and mentoring programs. Corporations know that if they invest in their employees, they will raise up their own leaders from within and build strong morale at the same time. A happy and fulfilled workforce will produce more and do so with a positive attitude. Ministries are beginning to see the same benefits that the business world has been putting into practice and are building into their budget the resources to pour back into their staff and pay off in dividends.

While it may seem like a new trend, the reality is that development is part of what it means to be human. As image-bearers, people weren't meant to be stagnant. We were meant to grow and move forward.

Growth is a given in the life of a Christian. In his second letter to the Corinthians, Paul wrote: "We all, with unveiled faces, are looking as in a mirror at the glory of the Lord and are being transformed into the same image from glory to glory; this is from the Lord who is the Spirit" (2 Cor. 3:18).

When the Holy Spirit works in our hearts to turn darkness to light, we are made new. But we are not made whole. Right now, on this side of heaven, we live in the tension of this already/not-yet reality. We are already completely justified by

> Growth is a given in the life of a Christian.

Christ but not yet fully sanctified. We rely on God's promise that one day when we see Jesus face-to-face, we will be fully transformed into the image of Christ. But right now, as we daily walk by faith, the Holy Spirit incrementally shapes us into who we were created to be. As Donald Whitney writes in *Spiritual Disciplines for the Christian Life*: "Although God will grant Christlikeness to us when Jesus returns, until then He intends for us to grow toward it."[8]

Our ultimate goal as individuals is to be like Jesus. Our ultimate goal as the church is to join in His mission to make disciples, taking the gospel to the ends of the earth. Everything we do in some way seeks that end, and it shows us that our work is never in vain. Our confidence comes from something outside of us because we know that all of the developmental tools He allows in our lives are ultimately being used by Him to equip us for every good work (Heb. 13:21). Our gifts and talents, our desires and loves, are all for something bigger than ourselves—specifically, His kingdom purposes. This means that not only is He maturing us when we don't see it, but we can pursue personal growth because He has given us the freedom and power to develop into who He has called us to be or to move forward into where He has called us to go.

> Our ultimate goal as individuals is to be like Jesus. Our ultimate goal as the church is to join in His mission to make disciples, taking the gospel to the ends of the earth. Everything we do in some way seeks that end, and it shows us that our work is never in vain.

Growth as a Leader

For a long time, I struggled with the idea of leadership. Often as women, we feel reluctant to pursue leadership or even desire it. We're hesitant and uncertain if developing in this way is biblical and appropriate for our gender. Scripture addresses roles in the home and the church, and there are specific callings for husbands and church elders that include leadership in those spheres, but that does not mean that all Christians should not grow in every area, including how to best steward our gifts and influence.

As Christians, we don't have a choice between being a leader or a follower. We are both. We follow Him in full submission. We submit to the authorities in our lives. But we also remember Paul's words about disciple-making: "Imitate me, as I also imitate Christ" (1 Cor. 11:1). We didn't join the family of God to live a life of inaction. We live a life on mission. We all live lives of influence, intended to point to the gospel. That makes all of us, to some extent, leaders.

> As Christians, we don't have a choice between being a leader or a follower. We are both.

Developing in the area of leadership can often be intimidating because we believe that, by definition, leaders must be in the spotlight, must be in charge, or must have some level of decision-making power. Leadership often means servanthood and quiet influence. Some of the best leaders I know might not have described their roles that way, but their examples pointed a way for others.

Lottie Moon was a missionary to China in the nineteenth century who built a body of work over years of difficult service. Her devotion to the people she reached was a driving force in her life. As she served them over a span of nearly forty years, she wrote letters back to the churches at home imploring them to support the work overseas. She sparked a movement of both financial and prayer support for missions around the world that continues today. As a woman, she leveraged her leadership for a higher cause. Now, over a century later, support for the international missions movement continues to thrive because of faithful influence and service.

When we grow as Christian women, we also grow as leaders and disciple-makers through the gifts the Lord has given us and the tasks that He has called us to. Spiritual growth and leadership growth are not mutually exclusive. Development does not require us to pull ourselves up by our bootstraps. Development comes when we show up and let the Lord shape us into who He has called us to be.

Know God

When I began my first communications job, I experienced imposter syndrome. Imposter syndrome occurs when we believe in our minds that we are unqualified or undeserving of the position we are in, and that soon, our coworkers or supervisors will discover that we don't have what it takes to fulfill the job requirements. In a sense, I felt like an imposter in the role I filled.

This is a common experience for many, but especially for women. There are many tips and tricks for battling imposter syndrome, often originating in self-coaching and esteem-building principles. Although these may offer some help, apart from Christ, they can't get to the ultimate root problem of this fear because the truth must be cultivated from beyond what we tell ourselves *about ourselves*. The world encourages us to say, "I've got this," and to see our own qualities and abilities as sufficient. But from the start, we must build our foundation on what God has done and has said about us.

> Development does not require us to pull ourselves up by our bootstraps. Development comes when we show up and let the Lord shape us into who He has called us to be.

Before personal or career development, spiritual development must take priority. It can be a great temptation to let our ambitions and interests take over and to believe that our first pursuit is to know more about our area of expertise or to know some new organizational principles that we haven't heard before. These are good things, but they aren't of first importance.

We must pursue transformation and personal maturity, which comes from the Word of God and connection to Him. Character and integrity are the most important assets of any worker, and for the believer, those can only be truly and ultimately cultivated through the transforming work of the Holy Spirit.

> Character and integrity are the most important assets of any worker, and for the believer, those can only be truly and ultimately cultivated through the transforming work of the Holy Spirit.

Spiritual disciplines such as prayer, fasting, Scripture meditation, and worship are gifts from God to His church as ways to stay connected to Him and grow in relationship with Him. The presence of the Holy Spirit lives in us, sanctifying us and making us into His image. When my husband was a pastor, he would often ask our congregation, "I know you know about Him, but do you truly know Him?" These gifts are ways in which we abide in Him to truly know the One who is alive in our hearts.

Knowing Him is foundational to life in this world. As we build that foundation, it is helpful for personal development to know ourselves and how He made us. We are each unique and have been given particular gifts and callings to serve the kingdom and the body of Christ. Knowing how He has created you and wired your interests, talents, and loves can help you grow into the good works you have been called to.

Know Yourself

As a child, I lived in a family of athletes. My father had played college football and spent his career in sports administration, my mother had played high school basketball, and my brother played baseball from Little League until the day he became a full-time coach himself. My day-to-day life usually encountered a ball and a scoreboard at some point. To most people, it would seem I was destined to be great on the court or the field, right? Not so fast.

I was uncoordinated, unbalanced, inflexible, and all-around terrible at almost everything I tried. Not only that, but it took me several years to admit that I really didn't like sports very much. I enjoyed the ballpark and the football stadium because it was familiar and the people I loved were there. But there are legendary family stories about important games, with the scores down to the wire, and while the crowds were on their feet I was crouched down on the bleachers with my nose in a book. As far as I was concerned, the game might be important, but the mystery that Nancy Drew was about to solve was much more crucial. It makes for a funny story, but it was also quite telling.

I reached a point when I had to recognize that I loved being around sports because I loved my family, and it was where they were. But I wasn't built for sports myself, and that was alright. I began to pour my energies into other activities at school, the things I truly loved and enjoyed. And it changed my trajectory because where I had failed miserably at throwing a ball, I thrived at delivering lines on the stage. The important factor was that my parents recognized I had different gifts and interests, and I recognized this as well. In order to pursue personal development well, you must know who you are.

Knowing yourself means understanding your strengths and your weaknesses, your struggles and insecurities, as well as your talents and loves. Some of the best ways to discover this come from asking those who know you best and who want to see you flourish. Also, self-reflection can be beneficial, not just regarding your current season and circumstances, but more broadly, your life as a whole. Most of the opportunities that have been best for me have involved hobbies and interests that began in my teenage years. This insight has helped me to hone in on where I should spend my time and energy now.

Finally, assessments aren't necessarily the final word, but they can be helpful in identifying areas for growth and investment. Organizations utilize various tools, such as StrengthsFinder, Working Genius, or Predictive Index. They all answer different questions, but each can be helpful in its own way. If you don't have access to more formalized tests, a basic spiritual gifts inventory can still bring great insight.

Take Initiative

After you have assessed areas of gifting or areas for improvement, pursue the development opportunities that are in front of you. These may include opportunities in your workplace, but they may be things that you have to seek out alone. One of the greatest insights I have received came from a leader who I worked with and admired, Selma Wilson. Selma would encourage women: "Own your own development." Her point was that we can often spend so much time waiting for someone to come and invest in us or tell us how to grow, that we miss the opportunities right in front of us. We have a wealth of knowledge and wisdom that we can access if we will only take the initiative to start learning.

Another way of thinking about this is self-leadership. We can determine areas of potential growth and begin pursuing them today. There are many options for growth and development, some at minimal financial cost. These are only a few considerations:

Read widely. I keep multiple books going at once from a variety of genres. Some are books on spiritual growth and sanctification. Some are on personal development. Others are biographies of missionaries, leaders, and historical figures. Learning from the stories of others can bring powerful wisdom and can demonstrate the beauty of God's work in the world and in the lives of people. Even great fiction can bring tremendous insight, with sometimes a single sentence staying with me and making me better.

Listen to others. Find the people you want to learn from and seek them out. Listen to them in person if they are near you. Ask them questions if you are able. Watch how they handle situations and reflect on what you have learned. If they aren't nearby, use technology to your advantage. With the advent of podcasts, YouTube, and other video resources for development, teachers and distant mentors can be accessed from the comforts of home. Whether near or far, seek out those who have something to teach and listen to them.

Stay current. We will always need to be learners because things are always changing. God doesn't change. Truth doesn't change. Our values don't change. But the areas in which we live and work may change in terms of technological advances, best practices in methodology, new products and markets, or platforms and delivery methods. Keeping up with current events and trends can help, whatever field you are in, as you prepare to bring your best into it.

> We will always need to be learners because things are always changing.

Learn wherever you are. Sometimes you may be in a season that isn't where you would ultimately like to be, but even there, learning opportunities can still be available to you. When I was an executive assistant, I wanted to learn whatever my boss was learning. When the president sent articles for the executive leadership team to read, I made a copy for myself to read as well. I knew that learning about the work we did would only help me serve my boss in even greater ways and would also help me understand our work more. When the day came that I had greater opportunities, I had gained a knowledge that I would not have if I had just made a copy for my boss and moved on. This came from seeing an opportunity to learn where I was and taking it.

Keep growing in the dry spells. In the cycles of our work, there will always be dry seasons. I have had two of them, one particularly difficult when I wasn't certain if I would ever be called to contribute again. I was discouraged and not sure where to even turn my efforts. I had a great friend who spoke clear and direct truths to me, pulling me out of the despair I was in. She reminded me that the Lord had placed me in that season and that He was preparing me for whatever would come next, which would be His best. She exhorted me to receive the time of rest and use it to prepare. She encouraged me to lean into creativity and journal my ideas, even if nothing ever came from them. I remember during that time I came up with an idea for a book that I never wrote, but the process of mapping it out actually gave me a great blueprint for the next role I was called to. The Lord was preparing me for the next stage, and I didn't even realize it in the moment. When you pursue growth, nothing is wasted.

> When you pursue growth, nothing is wasted.

Look to people who are good at what they do. Once I was preparing to attend a conference that focused on the arts, and I had to choose a breakout session. I asked a friend for counsel on which session to attend, and he advised me to go to a session on the experience of songwriting. I was a bit surprised and asked, "Why would I do that? I'm not a songwriter." He said something that has never left me: "Never underestimate the power of listening to someone who is really good at what they do, especially when they talk about how they do it." I had never considered this, but it struck me enough to take the advice and sign up for the session. That day, I was greatly blessed by all three panelists and received much joy from listening to them discuss their passion. But beyond that, one of the songwriters shared a lesson from his experiences and processes that was so applicable to my field that I still use it today when doing my work. I learned a valuable lesson. Learning from people in my area is highly beneficial. Learning from people in other areas who have mastered their craft can often be just as beneficial.

In 2010, Sheryl Sandberg gave women in the business world a new battle cry, and it stuck. She wasn't the first to encourage some version of female empowerment, and she wouldn't be the last. But her message resonated with a generation of young women that she called to "lean in."[9] Sandberg's groundbreaking work kicked off a nationwide conversation about what it meant to give it your all in order to have it all.

There are plenty of spaces for critique of Sandberg's work, beginning with the argument that women can't really have it all, particularly not in the same life season. Being human means that we are finite creatures, broken by sin after the fall. In this state, no one can have it all, nor should they. Beyond that, Sandberg's encouragement toward hard work is not in itself bad. Industriousness, career growth, and sometimes even advancement, can be good things. The question we must ask is: To what end?

We give ourselves to grow and serve the world around us, but as Christians, we are always giving ourselves to something bigger than ourselves because we know that we live in His kingdom here on earth. We pursue development in the areas we love for a greater purpose. We do our work to make His name known, even to the ends of the earth. We join in a mission that has already been promised, for a victory that has already been won.

> We give ourselves to grow and serve the world around us, but as Christians, we are always giving ourselves to something bigger than ourselves because we know that we live in His kingdom here on earth.

We do our work unto the Lord, knowing that He is shaping us into the image of His Son as we make disciples in the power of the gospel. Growth will happen, but it is preparing us to be an influence for Him. All work is kingdom work, and when He develops us it is ultimately for His purposes.

Reflection Questions

1. How do you prioritize spiritual growth before personal development?

2. Looking back over your life, can you identify ways in which the Lord has created and developed you for His work?

Conclusion

Let Your Light Shine

A Note from Courtney Moore

LET YOUR LIGHT SHINE. Words spoken by Jesus Himself in His famous Sermon on the Mount (Matt. 5:16). Words recorded from His first-century lips, from the overflow of His heart, meant for you even today.

Hear Him say it again, this time specifically to you: *Let your light shine, beloved daughter.*

In this, I hear His heart of love, His invitation for you to join Him in something bigger than yourself: a work of His, a global mission that He welcomes His child to participate in.

Did you notice the verb? *Let.*

It's a command. He wants you to allow yourself to shine. You don't have to hold back. You don't have to purposely keep your light dim for fear that the way you shine will be too bright for those around you to handle. If He's calling you to it, trust that He knows all the circumstances surrounding you. Believe that as you give yourself permission to fan your flame brighter, He will take care of all the details you can't control anyway. You need only keep your eyes on Him and follow Him step-by-step in faith.

He knows what awaits you on the other side of each step. It's the joy of His presence as you lean on Him with each stride. It's the good of your neighbor and the glory of your Father. This is the purpose of not only your work, but your life. *So, let your light shine.*

> He knows what awaits you on the other side of each step. It's the joy of His presence as you lean on Him with each stride. It's the good of your neighbor and the glory of your Father. This is the purpose of not only your work, but your life.

In 1942, Dorothy Sayers, contemporary of C. S. Lewis, gave an address in the town of Eastbourne, England, entitled, "Why Work?" In it, she compelled her listeners to work with excellence unto the Lord and to view their work as something sacred. She called them to shine their light as an offering of worship to God. She says,

> Work is not primarily a thing one does to live but the thing one lives to do. It is,

or it should be, the full expression of the worker's faculties, the thing in which he finds spiritual, mental, and bodily satisfaction, and the medium in which he offers himself to God.[10]

Dorothy Sayers's desire for workers is my heart for you. I pray that because of reading this book, you would truly view your life as integrated and whole, spent solely for King Jesus. May your work and your life be an offering to God as worship, and may you leverage your unique potential for His glory.

Work is a constant, even when paid work is not. You have a calling to cultivate and subdue the world, making it more like Eden in every step forward you take. You have a part to play, joining in where God is already working, as vessels of His grace. Don't allow what God has stirred as you've read to subside, because work was a gift prior to the fall. Although it grew more complicated and thorny, it is good, and it is for your good.

I suggest that you take several action steps, most involving a journal:

- Revisit sentences or paragraphs God used to speak to you. Reflect in your journal about these insights. Write down your own thoughts about what that point meant to you in this season of your life. Is there any action step you should take from that?

- Write down Scripture verses that spoke most to you throughout the book. Look those up in your Bible and begin reading the surrounding context of those verses. What is God saying in that passage, and how does this connect with what He is calling you to do? Write down those thoughts, and again, discern how to apply this to your life.

- Most important, pray. Write out your prayers if this helps you stay focused. Talk with God about what you have learned. Tell Him you are willing to follow where He leads and ask Him to show you what your next steps should be.

- Invite your local church community into your story. You need trusted brothers and sisters in Christ who know you well to speak wisdom into your life. And they also need the encouragement you bring to them as you relate all that God is doing in your heart.

- Connect with Women & Work. We'd love for you to reach out to let us know how this book has impacted you. We'd also be honored to continue to resource you into your God-given calling through our various initiatives such as *The Women & Work Podcast*, book club, online articles and interviews, events, and more. Find us at womenwork.net.

Last, it has been my joy to serve you with this project. As we part, I pray Hebrews 13:20–21 over you, dear sister.

> Now may the God of peace, who brought up from the dead our Lord Jesus—the great Shepherd of the sheep—through the blood of the everlasting covenant, equip you with everything good to do his will, working in us what is pleasing in his sight, through Jesus Christ, to whom be glory forever and ever. Amen.

Notes

1. Gene Edward Veith Jr., "Masks of God," *Modern Reformation*, May 2, 2007, https://modernreformation.org /resource-library/articles/masks-of-god/.

2. All statistics in this paragraph come from Michele Parmelee, "Women Continuing to Face Alarmingly High Levels of Burnout, Stress in the 'New Normal' Of Work," *Forbes*, April 26, 2022, accessed July 2022, https://www.forbes .com/sites/deloitte/2022/04/26/women-continuing-to-face -alarmingly-high-levels-of-burnout-stress-in-the-new-normal-of -work/?sh=303824b5432e.

3. Wendy Wang and Brad Wilcox, *The Power of the Success Sequence for Disadvantaged Young Adults*, May 2022, accessed September 22, 2022, https://www.aei.org/wp-content/uploads/2022/05/successsequencedisadvantagedya-final.pdf?x91208.

4. Carolyn Custis James, *Half the Church: Recapturing God's Global Vision for Women* (Grand Rapids: Zondervan, 2010), 35.

5. Tish Harrison Warren, *Liturgy of the Ordinary: Sacred Practices in Everyday Life* (Downers Grove, IL: InterVarsity, 2016), 94.

6. "Donna Harris on Faith & Entrepreneurship," *The Faith & Work Podcast*, Season 8, Episode 1.

7. Brother Lawrence, *Practicing the Presence of God: With Spiritual Maxims* (Grand Rapids: Baker, 1967), 30.

8. Donald Whitney, *Spiritual Disciplines for the Christian Life* (Colorado Springs: NavPress, 2014), 2.

9. Sheryl Sandberg, *Lean In: Women, Work, and the Will to Lead* (New York: Alfred A. Knopf, 2013).

10. Dorothy Sayers, "Why Work?" originally from *Letters to the Diminished Church* (1942), PDF File, April 2020, 6. https://www1.villanova.edu/content/dam/villanova/mission/faith/Why%20Work%20by%20Dorothy%20Sayers.pdf.

Contributors

Hannah Anderson is an author and Bible teacher who lives in the Blue Ridge Mountains of Virginia, with her husband Nathan and three children. Her books include *Made for More*, *Humble Roots*, and *All That's Good*. Hannah's goal is to encourage believers to think deeply and broadly about how the gospel transforms every area of life.

Missie Branch serves as assistant dean of students to women and director of Graduate Life at Southeastern Baptist Theological Seminary in North Carolina. She is also currently a student there completing her graduate degree in Ethics, Theology, and Culture. Missie is married to Duce and they have four children. She is passionate about women seeing themselves as theologians and disciples first. Missie is a contributing author to *The Whole Woman: Ministering to Her Heart, Soul, Mind, and Strength* and cohost of the Women & Work Podcast. Currently, Missie is serving as the chairman of the Board of Trustees at Lifeway Christian Resources.

Portia Collins is a Christian Bible teacher, writer, and podcaster with a passion for sharing God's Word. Portia is also the founder of She Shall Be Called, a nonprofit women's ministry focused on Bible literacy. You can also catch her hosting two weekly podcasts: *Grounded*—a podcast/videocast from Revive Our Hearts—and *Sweet Tea with Jasmine & Portia*. Portia and her husband Mikhail have a daughter and currently make their home in the Mississippi Delta.

Elyse Fitzpatrick has an MA in Biblical Counseling from Trinity Theological Seminary. She has authored twenty-five books on daily living and the Christian life. Elyse loves to proclaim the good news of the gospel: Jesus, the Second Person of the Trinity, perfectly obeyed all the Law in our place, suffered in isolation and agony as punishment for our sin, died, and then rose again, all for our justification. Elyse is a frequent speaker at national conferences. She has been married for nearly fifty years and has three adult children and six really adorable grandchildren. Along with her husband Phil, Elyse attends Grace Bible Church in Escondido, California.

Joanna Meyer serves as Denver Institute for Faith & Work's director of public engagement, where she leads the events, hosts the *Faith & Work Podcast*, and founded the national initiative Women, Work, & Calling. Prior to joining the Institute, she worked in global telecom, nonprofit consulting, and campus ministry with Cru. She also served as associate faculty for Denver Seminary's leadership development program. Joanna has an MA in Social Entrepreneurship from Bakke Graduate University and graduated magna cum laude from the University of Colorado, Boulder. She lives in Aurora, Colorado.

Courtney Moore is the founder and president of the nonprofit Women & Work, as well as cohost of the *Women & Work Podcast*. She holds a BA in Religious Studies from the University of Mobile and an MA in Biblical Counseling from The Southern Baptist Theological Seminary. Courtney is passionate about seeing Jesus Christ honored by women as they steward their gifts and leverage their unique potential for His glory. She and Brent are the proud parents of three great kids and live in El Paso, Texas, where Brent is a pastor.

Jen Oshman has been in women's ministry for more than two decades on three continents. She's the author of *Enough about Me, Cultural Counterfeits*, and *Welcome*. Jen hosts a weekly podcast about cultural events and trends called *All Things*, and she is the mother of four daughters. Her family currently resides in Colorado, where they planted Redemption Parker.

Courtney Powell holds a Bachelor of Music with an emphasis in Christian studies from Union University and an MA in Church Ministry from The Southern Baptist Theological Seminary. In addition to being an Operations Consultant for a nonprofit, she also serves as the director of ministry content for Women & Work, where she helps to create and promote content that encourages and inspires women to use their gifts for the advancement of the kingdom. She lives with her husband and three daughters in Arvada, Colorado, where her husband serves on staff with Storyline Church.

Courtney Reissig is a writer and Bible teacher living in Little Rock, Arkansas. She is the author of numerous books and Bible studies including *Teach Me to Feel: Worshiping Through the Psalms in Every Season of Life* and a forthcoming Bible study on the covenants. Courtney and her husband are the proud parents of four sons, and together they serve at Immanuel Baptist Church in Little Rock, Arkansas, where she is also the Discipleship Content Director.

Faith Whatley is the former director of adult ministry at Lifeway Christian Resources. For twenty-five years, she led and directed women's ministry serving churches all over the country. In 2019, Faith began to step back from her responsibilities and assumed the role of director of strategic partnerships. In 2021, she retired after almost thirty years at Lifeway. Faith has been married to Jim for thirty-five years and has two grown married children. Faith and Jim are blessed with three grandsons, Jameson, Hank, and Clyde, and are expecting their 4th grandson. They spend most of their time on Center Hill Lake, golfing, and keeping grandkids.

Amy Whitfield is executive director of communications at The Summit Church in Raleigh-Durham. Prior to that, she served in various roles within the Southern Baptist Convention for twenty years. She coauthored the book *SBC FAQs: A Ready Reference* and is cohost of the podcast *SBC This Week*. In 2019, she helped launch the SBC Women's Leadership Network, and she serves on the board of directors of Women & Work. Amy and her husband Keith have two children and live in Wake Forest, North Carolina.